STANLEY COMPLETE
ROOFS
& SIDING

Meredith® Books
Des Moines, Iowa

Stanley Complete Roofs & Siding
Editor: Larry Johnston
Copy Chief: Terri Frederickson
Copy Editor: Kevin Cox
Publishing Operations Manager: Karen Schirm
Senior Editor, Asset and Information Manager: Phillip Morgan
Edit and Design Production Coordinator: Mary Lee Gavin
Editorial and Design Assistant: Renee E. McAtee
Book Production Managers: Pam Kvitne,
    Marjorie J. Schenkelberg, Rick von Holdt, Mark Weaver
Imaging Center Operator: Ben Anderson
Contributing Copy Editor: Don Gulbrandsen
Contributing Proofreaders: Julia Bardwell, Ellen Bingham,
    Cheri Madison
Indexer: Donald Glassman
Other Contributors: Janet Anderson

**Additonal Editorial Contributions from
    Greenleaf Publishing**
Project Editor: Dave Toht
Writer: Steve Cory
Graphic Designer: Rebecca Anderson
Copy Editor: Barbara Webb
Photography: Dan Stultz, Stultz Photography; Steve Vento,
    Vento Photography, Inc.; Rebecca Anderson
Illustrator: Ian Worpole

Meredith® Books
Editor in Chief: Gregory H. Kayko
Executive Director, Design: Matt Strelecki
Managing Editor: Amy Tincher-Durik
Executive Editor/Group Manager: Benjamin Allen
Senior Associate Design Director: Tom Wegner
Marketing Product Manager: Brent Wiersma

Editorial Director: Linda Raglan Cunningham
Executive Director, Marketing: Kevin Kacere
Executive Director, New Business Development: Todd M. Davis
Executive Director, Sales: Ken Zagor
Director, Operations: George A. Susral
Director, Production: Douglas M. Johnston
Director, Marketing & Publicity: Amy Nichols
Business Director: Jim Leonard

Vice President and General Manager: Douglas J. Guendel

Meredith Publishing Group
President: Jack Griffin
Executive Vice President: Karla Jeffries

Meredith Corporation
Chairman of the Board: William T. Kerr
President and Chief Executive Officer: Stephen M. Lacy

In Memoriam: E. T. Meredith III (1933–2003)

Thanks to: ABC Supply Co., Inc.; Alcoa; Alside; CertainTeed
Corporation; Devin Devaney; EcoStar, a division of Carlisle
SynTec; Met-Tile; Arthur P. Murphy; MonierLifetile LLC; Royal
Group Technologies Limited; Daniel Vejr; Versico, Inc.; Wagner

All of us at Meredith® Books are dedicated to providing you
with the information and ideas you need to enhance your home
and garden. We welcome your comments and suggestions
about this book. Write to us at:
    Meredith Corporation
    Meredith Books
    1716 Locust St.
    Des Moines, IA 50309-3023

If you would like more information on other Stanley products,
call 1-800-STANLEY or visit us at: www.stanleyworks.com.
Stanley® and the notched rectangle around the Stanley
name are registered trademarks of The Stanley Works and
subsidiaries.

Note to the Readers: Due to differing conditions, tools, and
individual skills, Meredith Corporation assumes no responsibility
for any damages, injuries suffered, or losses incurred as a
result of following the information published in this book.
Before beginning any project, review the instructions carefully,
and if any doubts or questions remain, consult local experts
or authorities. Because codes and regulations vary greatly,
you always should check with authorities to ensure that your
project complies with all applicable local codes and regulations.
Always read and observe all of the safety precautions provided
by manufacturers of any tools, equipment, or supplies, and
follow all accepted safety procedures.

CONTENTS

Reference charts 4
How to use this book 5

PLANNING FOR ROOFING   6

Choosing roofing 8
Understanding your roof 12
Keeping out the water 14
Ordering the roofing 16
Other materials 18
Preparing the site 20
Working safely 22
Roofing tools 26

INSTALLING ASPHALT SHINGLES   28

Preparing for the job 30
Roofing over existing shingles 32
Tearing off old shingles 36
Repairing sheathing 38
Applying underlayment 40
Installing pre-shingle flashings 42
Installing three-tab shingles 44
Installing valleys and
    chimney flashing 50

INSTALLING OTHER ROOFING   54

Cedar shakes 56
Vertical metal roofing 62
Faux tiles 66
Tile roofs 68
Modified-bitumen roofing 74
Roll roofing 80

ROOF REPAIRS   82

Identifying problems 84
Spot and emergency repairs 86
Replacing shingles and shakes 88
Repairs to a flat roof 90
Flashing repairs 92
Chimney repairs 94
Venting an attic 96
Installing attic vents 98

PREPARING FOR SIDING   102

Understanding siding
    and framing 104
Flashing around windows
    and doors 105
Choosing siding materials 106
Removing siding and
    repairing sheathing 110
Applying felt or building paper 112
Applying trim 114

INSTALLING SIDING   118

Installing horizontal wood
    lap siding 120
Fiber-cement lap siding 126
Tongue-and-groove siding 128
Installing vinyl siding 130
Installing siding shingles 136
Shingle panels 142
Rain-screen siding 143
Board-and-batten siding 144
Installing panel siding 146

REPAIRING SIDING   152

Sealing joints 154
Paint problems 156
Prepping for house painting 158
Painting a house 160
Repairing lap siding 164
Repairs to other wood siding 166
Repairing vinyl siding 168
Repairing aluminum siding 170
Repairing stucco 172

GUTTERS AND EAVES   174

Fascia and soffit repairs 176
Gutter repairs 178
Installing gutters 182

GLOSSARY   186

INDEX   188

REFERENCE CHARTS

CAULKS AND SEALANTS

TYPE	PROPERTIES
Latex, acrylic latex, vinyl latex	Water-base, easy to apply, low odor. Adheres well to most building materials. Wide range of products intended for many uses, interior and exterior; choose one with qualities suited to your job. Paintable when cured.
Silicone	More difficult to apply neatly, mild odor when uncured, requires solvent clean up. Adheres poorly to wood but well to glass, ceramic tile, metal, other nonporous surfaces. Most cannot be painted. Strong, water resistant for many materials.
Synthetic rubber	Solvent base makes many unsuitable for interior use. Can be applied to wet or cold surfaces. Stretches easily to maintain seal. Adheres to most building materials. Good for roofing and siding. Usually paintable.
Polyurethane	Difficult to apply neatly, mild odor, potential health hazard. High abrasion resistance makes it best for floors or porch surfaces. Weather-resistant, flexible and paintable. Better to use safer sealants unless polyurethane's properties are essential.
Butyl rubber	Messy to apply and may look unattractive. Highest water resistance of any caulk; remains flexible to maintain seal between surfaces that may move. Best for gutters, flashings, and foundations.
Modified-silicone polymer	New technology, relatively expensive. Easy to apply, cures quickly. Can be applied in wet or cold, durable, adheres well to most building materials. Flexible and paintable with water-base paint.
Water-base foam	Fills larger gaps than caulk. Relatively low expansion rate makes it easy to apply. Seals out air, but many aren't water-resistant. Has slight insulation value. Soft surface of cured material is easily damaged.
Polyurethane foam	Fills large gaps. Expands as it cures; can be difficult to apply neatly. Various products are usually specified as low-, medium-, or high-expansion formulas. Dense surface when cured, resists moisture and has some insulation value.

METRIC CONVERSIONS

U.S. UNITS TO METRIC EQUIVALENTS			METRIC EQUIVALENTS TO U.S. UNITS		
To Convert From	Multiply by	To Get	To Convert From	Multiply by	To Get
Inches	25.4	Millimeters	Millimeters	0.0394	Inches
Inches	2.54	Centimeters	Centimeters	0.3937	Inches
Feet	30.48	Centimeters	Centimeters	0.0328	Feet
Feet	0.3048	Meters	Meters	3.2808	Feet
Yards	0.9144	Meters	Meters	1.0936	Yards
Square inches	6.4516	Square centimeters	Square centimeters	0.1550	Square inches
Square feet	0.0929	Square meters	Square meters	10.764	Square feet
Square yards	0.8361	Square meters	Square meters	1.1960	Square yards
Acres	0.4047	Hectares	Hectares	2.4711	Acres
Cubic inches	16.387	Cubic centimeters	Cubic centimeters	0.0610	Cubic inches
Cubic feet	0.0283	Cubic meters	Cubic meters	35.315	Cubic feet
Cubic feet	28.316	Liters	Liters	0.0353	Cubic feet
Cubic yards	0.7646	Cubic meters	Cubic meters	1.308	Cubic yards
Cubic yards	764.55	Liters	Liters	0.0013	Cubic yards

To convert from degrees Fahrenheit (F) to degrees Celsius (C), first subtract 32, then multiply by 5/9.

To convert from degrees Celsius to degrees Fahrenheit, multiply by 9/5, then add 32.

HOW TO USE THIS BOOK

Roofing and siding installation are realistic do-it-yourself projects, but either can be challenging. For example, installing new siding may require demolition skills as well as an understanding of framing. You will have to install weatherproof flashing and finished-looking trim at corners and around doors and windows. Actually installing the siding material itself is the easy part; preparation and finishing touches require the most skill and patience.

Maintenance and repair of roofing and siding are important too—gaps or leaks can allow damage to the structure of your home or its contents. And they increase energy costs. Integrity of flashings, caulking, and roofing or siding materials themselves must be maintained. Some of this work can be time-consuming, but most is not complicated.

Hiring contractors for roofing or siding jobs can cost a lot. So handling your own repair, upgrade, or installation offers a chance to build some sweat equity.

Cutting the job down to size
This book is designed to provide you with clear, illustrated steps so you can handle many roofing and siding jobs yourself—and keep some remodeling money in your own pocket. For a good example of how this book takes challenging tasks and breaks them down into manageable stages, jump ahead to the chapter "Installing Asphalt Shingles" beginning on page 28. You'll find that even if you decide to tear off the old roofing, all the procedures involved in the job are shown in simple steps. Following the instructions will result in a completed project you can be proud of.

Getting started
If you are contemplating new roofing or siding get off to a good start with either "Planning for Roofing" beginning on page 6 or "Preparing for Siding" starting on page 102. These chapters show the range of materials available and help you decide which is right for your project. They will also help you assess what the job will involve. Other chapters show how to install and repair various kinds of roofing and siding and how to install, maintain, and repair gutters and downspouts.

Tailored to your situation
Stanley Complete Roofs & Siding is essentially two books in one. Whether your primary project is roofing or siding, you'll find the information you need to get the job done. And because your home likely has unique characteristics, you may run into situations unlike those shown in the step-by-step projects. When you encounter a difference, check the lower half of the page for boxes that provide more information. Boxes labeled "What If…?" present alternative solutions that you can apply to your specific situation.

You'll also find valuable expert advice and inside information on new tools and products in the "Stanley Pro Tip" boxes. "Safety First" boxes offer reminders on how to keep your project injury-free. Additional boxes and sidebars offer detailed information that can move your project along.

Knowing your limits
In addition to helping you through projects one step at a time, this book provides an overview that will tell you what work is—or isn't—within your do-it-yourself comfort zone. You may decide that for a particular project your best role will be that of knowledgeable project manager. For the price of a roll of adhesive flashing you have a book that will add to your knowledge base, putting you in a position to farm out the tasks you don't have the time or skills to take on.

SAFETY FIRST
Keep your job site comfortable and injury free

Repairing, upgrading, and installing roofing and siding involve tools and techniques that require good safety habits. Use these guidelines to keep the job injury free:

■ Set goals, allow enough time to complete them, and take breaks. Nothing puts you at risk quite like fatigue and frustration.

■ Make your workplace comfortable. Keep tools spread out but close at hand. Invest in a good tool belt or bucket belt and put each tool back in the same place after using it.

■ Wear gloves when handling framing lumber, doing demolition, working with glass, or cutting metal. When lifting, remember that gloves make you strong—they increase your grip and lessen discomfort.

■ Save your knees—wear knee pads for any task that calls for kneeling. Your stamina and pleasure in the job will be greatly improved.

■ Wear a respirator or high-quality dust mask when doing demolition work, sawing, insulating, or sanding—any activity that produces airborne dust.

■ Eye protection is a must when sawing, working with glass, drilling metal—any activity that may send hazardous bits of debris flying.

■ When working at heights, use a strong ladder. Shim the legs to keep the ladder from rocking and obey the warnings on the ladder about not using the last couple of steps. Where possible, make a work platform—you'll not only improve your safety but your workmanship as well.

■ Running to the home center or hardware store in the middle of a project is an irritant you can avoid. Make sure you have all the necessary materials and tools on hand before you start a project. Make tool and material lists and check them before you start work.

PLANNING FOR ROOFING

Often a roofing job is fairly simple to map out. For example, if you will simply reroof over existing asphalt shingles with the same type of shingles, the decisions are few and easy. However, if you need to tear off the old shingles or if you want to change the look of your roof, you will need to make several practical and aesthetic decisions.

Choosing materials

Choose the roofing material—shingles, tiles, or sheets—that best complements your home's architectural style. Practical considerations, such as fire and other local codes, the slope of the roof, and the way the roof was built, may limit your choices. To be safe, use a material that has proven durable in your area. Typically longer-lasting material will cost more. How long you plan to live in your home will bear upon your decision. This chapter will guide you through the choices.

Do it yourself or hire a pro?

This book will equip you to install a variety of roofing types. However, before you dive into a roofing project, consider whether you are really up to the task. This is physically demanding work and can be dangerous as well. Read through the sections on preparing the site and working safely (pages 20–25), then peruse the instructions later in the book for the type of roofing you will install. One important consideration: Can you reroof over existing shingles or will you need to tear off the old roofing?

If you do the work yourself, buy or rent tools that will make the job easier. A power nailer (page 27) is usually well worth the cost, for instance. Also enlist strong people to help load the roofing and move it around the roof. Use safety equipment suitable for the slope of your roof.

If you hire a pro, choose one who is licensed and bonded to guarantee satisfactory work. Be sure a contractor is insured so that you will not be liable if an accident occurs. A roofing contract should clearly state the start and completion dates; the price; materials, including underlayment; and a guarantee that your yard will not be damaged.

Choose a roofing material that best complements the architectural style of your home.

CHAPTER PREVIEW

Choosing roofing
page 8

Understanding your roof
page 12

Keeping out the water
page 14

Ordering the roofing
page 16

Color scheming
While the paint scheme of your home can often guide your color choice of your new roof, it may be best to choose neutral colors. Gray, white, or black roofing offers flexibility if you decide to change your color scheme.

To avoid timewasting trips to replenish supplies—and risk finding your particular style and color of shingle unavailable—take time to measure your roof carefully. You'll also be equipped to estimate your materials cost and upgrade (or downgrade) the style of shingle you choose.

Other materials
page 18

Preparing the site
page 20

Working safely
page 22

Roofing tools
page 26

CHOOSING ROOFING

Roofing can dramatically change the appearance of a home. If your existing roof is standard three-tab asphalt shingles, you can give the house a new look with architectural shingles or with concrete or metal tiles.

Practical considerations may limit your choices. Cedar shakes should be used only for roofs that are pitched at 4:12 or steeper (to determine your roof's slope, see page 17). Before choosing a heavy material like clay tile, check with local codes or a carpenter to make sure your roof structure will be strong enough. (Some clay-look tiles are actually much lighter than real clay.)

Check local building codes and zoning ordinances. Many neighborhoods permit only certain types of roofing to ensure that one house is not jarringly different in style from other homes on the block. Local fire codes may prohibit wood shakes or wood shingles. Nonwood roofing materials typically are rated for fire resistance. Roofing that has a Class A rating will withstand even a fire that originates in the house below. Class B roofing will resist only moderate exposure to fire from outside the home, and Class C roofing has only minimal fire resistance.

Check out the manufacturer's warranty. It is usually a good idea to buy roofing that is guaranteed for at least 30 years. Although 20 years (the typical guarantee for low-end roofing products) may seem like a long time, moderate savings may not be worth it. Remember, when you sell the house, the remaining life expectancy of the roof may affect how much a buyer will pay.

STANLEY PRO TIP

Algae and fungus protection

Some shingles come with a guarantee against fungus and algae. If you live in a damp climate, this can be a good choice. Often, however, the fungus and algae guarantee may be limited to only 10 years.

Composition shingles, made of asphalt or fiberglass, are the most common roofing choice because they are inexpensive and easy to install. The three-tab type is the most popular style, but you can also buy random-cutout shingles for a textured look or no-cutout shingles for a cleaner appearance.

Asphalt-based shingles are made with an asphalt base covered with crushed mineral granules. The result is a material that resists tearing but is sometimes prone to curling (also called fishmouthing). This type of shingle usually has a Class B or C fire rating.

Fiberglass shingles look like asphalt but are lighter. (Some shingles are made with both fiberglass and asphalt and may be referred to as "asphalt shingles.") They are less prone to curling than asphalt, though they do tear more easily and may split or crack after a few decades. Fiberglass shingles often have a Class A fire rating.

In most areas fiberglass is the more popular choice. Check with your local supplier to see which type performs best in your area.

Architectural shingles, also called laminated or dimensional shingles, are made by laminating a top layer (which is notched) onto a bottom layer (which is solid). This produces a textured look. With some types the top layer is a different color from the bottom layer. These are more expensive than standard asphalt or fiberglass shingles, but they last longer and are usually no more difficult to install.

Shingle warranty

The thicker and more durable the shingle, the longer the warranty. Warranties are limited and prorated, so if the shingles fail a couple of years before the expiration date, you will get only a small amount of money—usually not enough to make it worth the trouble to pursue a claim. Still the length of the warranty is a good predictor of how long shingles will last.

Roll roofing is made of the same material as asphalt or fiberglass shingles but comes in the form of 36-inch-wide rolls. It is not as thick as most shingles, so it usually has a short life expectancy. It is also not particularly attractive. However it can be a practical choice for a small, nearly flat roof or for a garden shed. If you install it in a double layer, it will last as long as standard shingles. Selvage-edged rolls are made for double-thickness installation, because they have granules only on half the width.

Wood shakes and shingles are made from cedar. Shakes are split, giving them a rough surface. Cedar shingles are sawn and have a smooth surface. Shakes and shingles graded No. 1 are made from cedar heartwood, so they resist rot well and are knot-free. Avoid using No. 2 or No. 3 shingles or shakes, which will not last well. Shakes and shingles may last anywhere from 25 to 50 years, depending on their exposure to the weather. Freezing rain is hard on them, as is intense sunlight. Applying a preservative can greatly extend their life.

Slate tiles are split from natural stone. Slate will usually last a long time and is highly resistant to fire, but it is expensive and difficult to install. Colors range from gray to green. Slate is usually applied on a roof with a steep slope. Walking on slate may crack it. Real slate should be installed by a professional roofer with slate experience. As an alternative consider look-alike metal or concrete tiles.

Metal tile-look roofing looks like the flatter type of clay tile but is far lighter and easier to install. It is sometimes installed directly onto roof rafters in new construction, but it can also be installed onto a standard sheathed roof. One warning: Metal roofing can be noisy during a heavy rainstorm.

Vertical metal roofing, once associated with commercial buildings, is now available in attractive colors ideal for residential applications. It has a sleek, modern look and is easy to install. Choose thicker panels, which will last longer; check the warranty. Copper vertical roofing is also long-lasting but expensive and difficult to install. Over time it will turn a verdigris color. Copper is available in a vertical or shingle look. It should be installed professionally.

Clay tiles may be scalloped (or S-shape), fairly flat, or ribbed. A genuine Spanish-style clay tile roof will last indefinitely. However it is very heavy; if your home was not originally framed for clay tile, it is probably not strong enough. Though credible faux tiles made of metal, concrete, or cement fiber are available, some people find that only real clay has the look they want. Clay tile must be installed by a professional.

Built-up roofing, also called a tar-and-gravel roof, is an older method of roofing a flat roof. However if you have an existing built-up roof, it often makes sense to reroof using the same method. Installation involves heating a large kettle of tar to skin-damaging temperatures, making this a job for pros only.

Concrete tiles (below) are made of portland cement, sand, and water. They are less expensive and easier to install than genuine clay and just as fire-resistant. However they are heavier than asphalt shingles, so consult with your local building department before installing them or you may damage the roof structure.

Modified bitumen and **EPDM (rubber) roofing** are now the most common choices for large flat (or nearly flat) roofs. They come in large sheets and are extremely strong and flexible. Some bitumen sheets have a granular surface while others are smooth; EPDM sheets are completely smooth. It is common to cover the smooth sheets with a layer of silver coating to improve durability and to make the roof reflect heat.

UNDERSTANDING YOUR ROOF

A well-built roof seals out water and directs it to gutters and downspouts, which carry the water away from the house. To perform well underlayment, flashings, and the roofing material must be installed correctly so water cannot seep under and damage the sheathing.

A roof also must provide ventilation so the attic does not overheat in the summer. Inadequate ventilation can cause moisture buildup in the attic, which will likely compromise the insulation. It can also cause ice dams, which can damage the roofing, sheathing, and framing. (See pages 96–101 for ways to vent an attic.)

Roof rafters and **trusses** rest on the top plates of the wall framing. If your roof has rafters they usually meet at a ridge board (or beam), a board that runs along the peak (as shown in the cutout for the ridge vent). A roof built with trusses usually has blocking pieces placed between trusses at the ridge. Trusses or rafter tails usually extend down past the house wall and are cut plumb at their ends. A fascia board is often attached to the rafter ends, and rain gutters are installed onto the fascia. The overhanging roof edge is called the eave; it is often covered on the underside with soffit boards that fit up against the house siding.

Sheathing covers the rafters or trusses. In an older home sheathing may be made of 1× boards. In newer homes sheathing is usually made of plywood or OSB (oriented strand board). Roofing felt, often called tar paper, provides the underlayment for the roof. The felt is usually stapled down, but sometimes roofing nails or specialty nails are used. Felt is necessary to provide a vapor barrier that protects the sheathing from condensation moisture. At the lower parts of the roof near the eaves, a self-adhesive membrane is usually applied instead of felt to provide added protection against ice dams.

Flashings are just as important as the roofing itself for sealing out rain and snow. They must be installed correctly so water cannot seep under them. Drip-edge flashing is designed for use at eaves and rakes (the ends of the roof). Usually the eave flashing is installed, then the underlayment, then the rake flashing. At a valley wide flashing is installed over two layers of underlayment and under the roofing. Plumbing vents have their own rubber flashing, which fits under the shingles at the top half and over the shingles at the bottom half. At the chimney there is a complicated arrangement of step flashing pieces, a cricket, and counterflashings, which must be correctly installed and sealed with roofing cement to keep water out of the structure.

Finally the **roofing** itself covers the underlayment and most of the flashings. Whichever type of roofing you apply, it must be installed so every piece overlaps the next lower piece, allowing water to flow down. Roofing nails or staples are almost all covered by another piece of roofing above. Where they are exposed they should be protected with roofing cement.

ROOF COMPONENTS

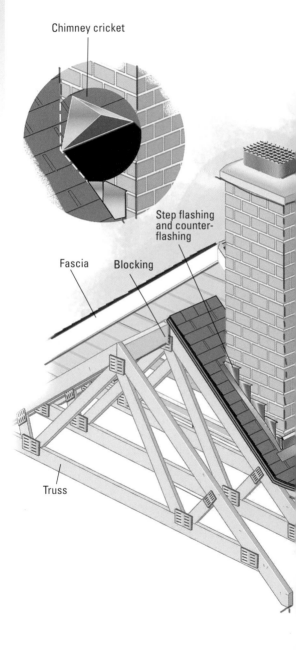

Chimney cricket

Step flashing and counter-flashing

Fascia

Blocking

Truss

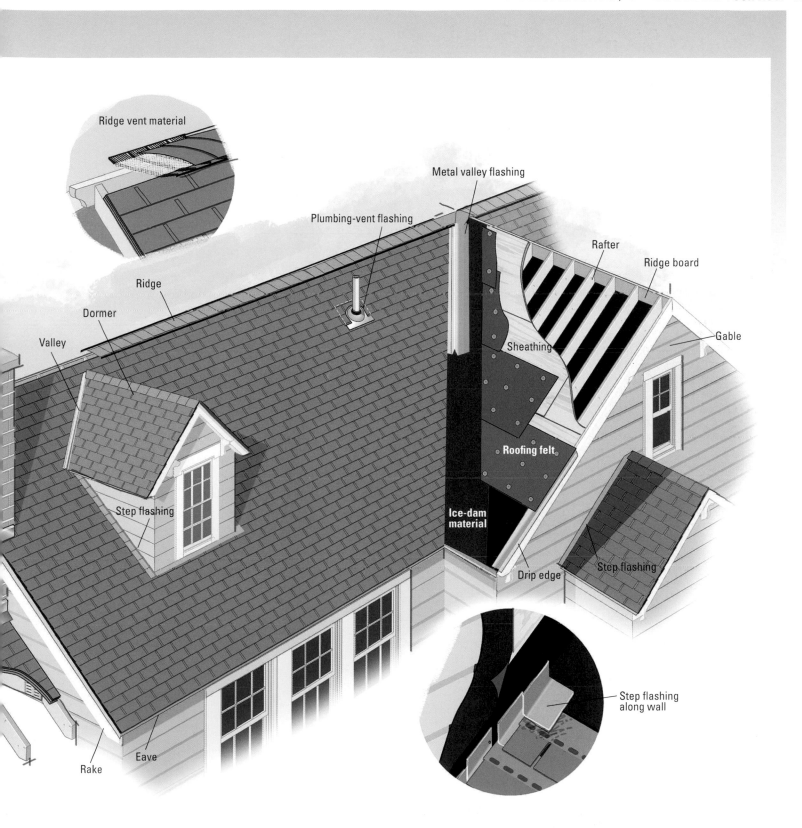

Ridge vent material

Metal valley flashing

Plumbing-vent flashing

Rafter

Ridge board

Ridge

Gable

Dormer

Sheathing

Valley

Roofing felt

Step flashing

Ice-dam material

Drip edge

Step flashing

Step flashing along wall

Rake

Eave

KEEPING OUT THE WATER

Keeping your home dry inside calls for covering the roof with the right materials and installing them in the right order. They must be firmly secured in such a way that fasteners are covered. (For advice about inspecting your roof for problems or conditions that could lead to leaks, see pages 84–85.)

Much of the process of applying roofing is straightforward, but there are many ways to get it wrong and produce a faulty roof. These pages show some of the trickier installations. Once you understand how the pieces should go together, installing them will be fairly easy. If you are ever uncertain how to proceed, consult with a professional roofer. A leak can cause serious and expensive damage to your home's interior, so it's worth any extra cost and effort to make sure that you are installing roofing correctly.

Eave and rake flashings make it difficult for water to seep under the roofing and underlayment, keeping the sheathing dry. Drip edge, also called roof-edge flashing, is installed at the rake and the eaves. The best arrangement is to attach the drip edge at the eaves directly to the sheathing. The underlayment (felt or waterproof membrane) goes over the eaves flashing, then the drip edge on the rake lies over the underlayment. The roofing's starter strip and the first course of shingles overhang the drip edge by ½ inch.

Counter-flashing

Step flashing

Base flashing

Flashing around a chimney is often a problem spot. If the flashing pieces are not installed tightly and correctly, water can seep in around the bricks and slowly damage the framing in the attic. In the usual arrangement a single piece of flashing runs across and wraps around the base of the chimney. Individual pieces of step flashing at the sides are installed along with the roofing; each piece rests on top of a lower shingle and under the next higher shingle.

At the upper side of the chimney (not visible), there is usually a "cricket"—a peaked roof that diverts water to the sides of the chimney (see page 53). The cricket can be plywood covered with flashing or roofing or it can be made entirely of metal flashing.

Counterflashing pieces, which overlap the other flashing pieces, are installed last. These must be tightly sealed against the chimney brick. This is often done by cutting grooves in the mortar and bending the flashing to slip into the grooves. The tops of the flashing pieces are often sealed with mortar, then roofing cement.

Visible valley flashing where two roofs meet is one common way to keep water flowing downward unobstructed. The flashing must be wide enough that water cannot seep under it and reach the sheathing. Attach it with cleats or nails driven at the outside edges so that only the heads capture the flashing. Nails driven through the flashing can lead to leaks. Sealing the shingle edges as shown keeps water from working its way underneath. (For closed or woven valleys, which cover the flashing or are applied without a flashing, see pages 50–53.)

Gutters must be firmly attached to the eave fascia and tucked under the roofing so water will run into and not behind them. Gutters must slope so water runs to a downspout, which carries water down and away from the foundation with the use of a downspout extender (shown). Upper parts fit into lower parts so that water does not seep out at the joints. Connect the joints with screws and seal them with gutter caulk. (For more on gutter maintenance and installation, see pages 178–185.)

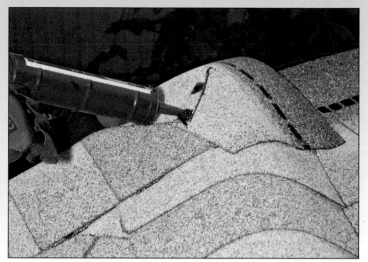

Overlapping shingles cover nails, sealing off leaks. Roof fasteners are usually covered by the shingle or tile above. The front edge of an asphalt shingle is held down with a thick dotted line of self-sealing adhesive on the shingle it rests on. Tiles and shakes are firm enough that they do not need their front edges fastened down. At the ridge and other places, you will end up with a couple of exposed nailheads. Cover these with roofing cement as shown.

Step flashing is installed where a roof meets a side wall at an angle. Step flashing must tuck under the house's siding or be protected by a counterflashing so water cannot seep behind the top edge of the flashing. Where the roof meets the front of a wall on a level line, wide L-shape drip-edge flashing is installed so it slips under the house's siding and rests on top of the roofing. At a corner like the one shown, a special piece of flashing should be custom-cut to make the transition. Self-adhesive flexible flashing can often be used in this situation. The house's siding should be cut at least ½ inch above the roof so that water cannot wick up into the siding.

Flashing around plumbing stacks is installed so that the upper half is covered with roofing and part of the lower half rests on top of roofing. You can easily visualize how rainwater will run over the roofing and the flashing, rather than under them. Similar flashing arrangements are used around skylights.

ORDERING THE ROOFING

You will order roofing and underlayment by the "square"—that is, 100 square feet. To estimate your needs, calculate the total square footage of your roof. For the most accurate measurement, you could actually go on the roof and measure each section, but that is often difficult and time-consuming. (If you can easily reach a gable to calculate your roof's pitch, or slope, see the method shown in the Pro Tip on the opposite page.)

More commonly, square footage is estimated by measuring from the ground and then making some simple calculations. The steps on this page show you how. (However you may need to climb up on the roof to measure any dormers or other protrusions.)

Once you have calculated your roof area, do not subtract for small obstructions such as chimneys or skylights. If you have dormers climb onto the roof and measure them or make a rough estimate. Add up all the roofing sections; add 10 percent for waste.

Arranging for delivery

It's not a good idea to leave bundles of shingles sitting on the roof for days so delay delivery until you are ready to roof. Watch the weather reports; you can't roof when it is raining. If the roofing will be delivered onto the roof (see opposite page), have it delivered after you have installed the flashings and underlayment, just before you will start roofing. If it will be delivered to your yard or driveway, have it arrive sooner.

If you have to move bundles around, do so safely; see page 21 for how to pick up and carry shingles. See page 23 for how to carry bundles up a ladder.

Measure from the ground

1 Sketch all the sections. Make rough outline drawings of all the roof's rectangular and triangular sections. These drawings do not have to be accurate. They may include the main roof, overhang sections, and dormers. Divide each section into simple squares, rectangles, and right triangles. For example, if a section is a rectangle with a triangular section at one end (like the roof over the entryway above), draw a line to divide it into a rectangle and a right triangle.

MAKING THE CALCULATIONS

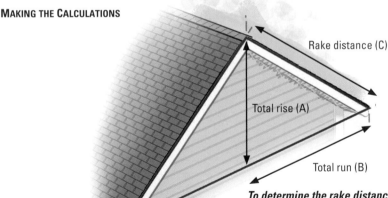

Once you have measurements from the ground as well as the roof pitch, you can estimate the square footage of the roof. First figure the roof's total rise: Multiply the unit rise (which would be 6 if you have a 6:12 pitch) by half the house's total width to the eaves, which is the base of the triangle. If your house is 24 feet wide, the base of this triangle is 12 feet. Multiply 12 times 6 (the unit rise for a 6:12 pitch) to get 72; this is the total rise in inches, so the total rise is 6 feet.

To determine the rake distance (the distance from the bottom of the eave to the top of the ridge), add the square of the total rise (A) plus the square of the total run (B). If the total rise is 6 feet, square that to get 36; if the total run is 12 feet, square that to get 144. Add them to get 180. Use a calculator to find the square root of 180, which is 13.4—the length of the rake in feet.

Now that you know the length of the rake (C), you can start to figure your roof sections by simply multiplying length times width. For instance, if a section of this house is 20 feet long, multiply 13.4 times 20 to get 268 square feet for that section.

2 Measure from the ground. Stand under the eaves or a gable and measure out from the house to get the overhang distance. Measure the length and width of the house and add the overhang dimensions where appropriate. Note these figures.

3 Estimate the roof pitch by using a ruler and a combination square. Use the bubble in the combination square to level the straightedge. Move the ruler to the 12-inch mark on the straightedge. Then slide the ruler up until it intersects the roofline. The number of inches up to the roofline is the rise. For instance, if the ruler shows 6 inches, your roof has a 6 in 12 rise (a 6:12 slope).

Up on the roof

Getting the shingles or tiles onto the roof can be a difficult part of the job; you may find yourself worn out before you even start applying them. Inquire about delivery options. If the roofing supplier can place the shingles onto the roof using a crane, that service may be worth the cost. Some companies use a conveyor-belt device to carry the bundles up to the roof.

STANLEY PRO TIP: **Capturing the roof slope**

To more accurately measure your slope, clasp a carpenter's level on top of the long leg of a framing square and hold the square against the roofline. Position the long (24-inch) leg of the square so that the 12-inch mark intersects the roofing. The square's short leg will show the rise. For instance, if you read 12 inches on the long leg and 6 inches on the short leg, the slope is 6:12.

Or place a 2-foot level on the roof, make sure it is horizontal, and measure up from the roof (using another level to make sure you are measuring plumb). Then divide the numbers in half.

OTHER MATERIALS

In addition to the roofing material, you will need several materials to complete the job. For most projects the list is fairly short: underlayment, flashing, fasteners, and roofing cement. However, you must make decisions regarding the type of materials.

Flashings

Metal flashings have been the most common type for many years. **Aluminum,** which will never rust, is generally preferred over galvanized steel, which can rust. **Copper flashing** is beautiful but expensive. **Vinyl** flashing products are gaining in popularity. They are easy to work with and do not crease easily, as do metal flashings. It is possible to make your own flashings by bending metal strips or rolls, but in nearly every case, you can buy preformed flashings that install easily and do the job well. Black, brown, white, and natural metal are the most common flashing colors.

If you have a valley and want to flash it open metal style (see pages 50–53), buy **valley flashing** made for the purpose. The best type has attaching cleats, so you don't have to drive nails through the flashing itself.

There are two basic types of **drip edge. T-shape** is stronger and will support roofing that overhangs the eaves. **L-shape** flashing is also common. You can use L-shape drip edge for the rake and T-shape drip edge for the eaves. **Cap drip edge** is ideal for sealing multiple layers of roofing.

For step flashing, you can buy prebent pieces or **blanks** that you bend yourself. For the counterflashing needed on chimneys (see page 94), use blanks or cut pieces from a roll of flashing.

Self-stick flexible flashing is more commonly used when installing windows and doors, but it can sometimes be used in difficult flashing situations, such as where a roof meets a wall.

You'll also need boot flashing, vent pipe flashing with rubber gaskets that simply slides onto the pipes to provide a watertight seal (see pages 48 and 93). You can buy boot flashing with metal or plastic flanges. Concrete tile installations require a lead sleeve-type flashing (see page 72). You'll probably need to buy that from a specialty building supplies dealer.

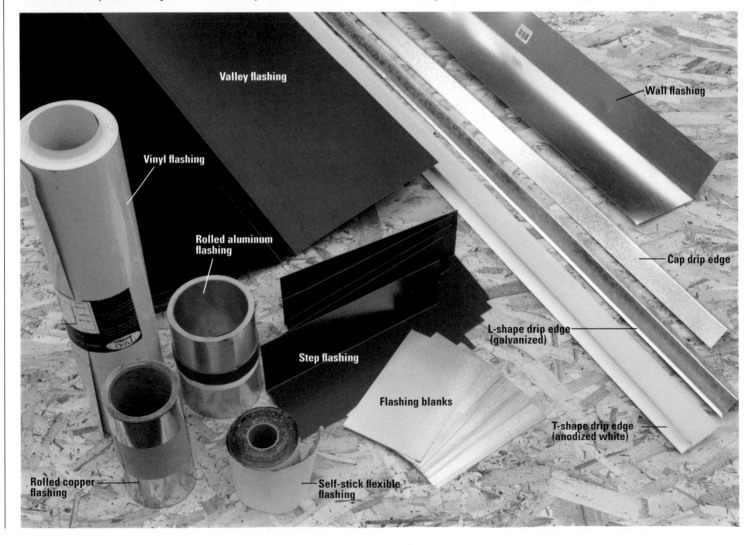

- Valley flashing
- Wall flashing
- Vinyl flashing
- Rolled aluminum flashing
- Cap drip edge
- Step flashing
- L-shape drip edge (galvanized)
- Flashing blanks
- T-shape drip edge (anodized white)
- Rolled copper flashing
- Self-stick flexible flashing

Coil roofing nails

2" nails

1¾" nails

Shake nails

Plastic-cap roofing
felt nails

1¼" nails

Wide-crown staples
for pneumatic nailer

Roofing nails
Buy nails that are long enough to completely poke through the sheathing; the length will depend on how thick the roofing is and how many layers of roofing there are. **Galvanized** nails are the most common choice for hand-nailing roofing. Use **aluminum nails** for attaching aluminum flashings, and copper nails for attaching copper flashings; if you mix metals, the nails or the flashing could corrode. **Nails with plastic caps** are sometimes used to attach underlayment in high wind areas. If you use a power nailer, buy roofing **nails in coils. Wide-crown staples** are also sometimes used with pneumatic nailers. **Nails for cedar shakes** or shingles have thin shanks and small heads.

Roofing cement
Thick roofing cement, which is either troweled on or applied with a caulk gun, is the most common type used in roofing. For an emergency patch you can apply **wet-surface cement** even while rain is coming down. **Liquid lap cement** is used for applying sheets of roll roofing.

Roofing felt
Often called tar paper, roofing felt is a critical component of a roof. Thirty-pound felt is twice as thick as 15-pound felt, making it more durable and less likely to wrinkle when you install it. Traditional felt is infused with asphalt; newer types are fiberglass reinforced for extra strength.

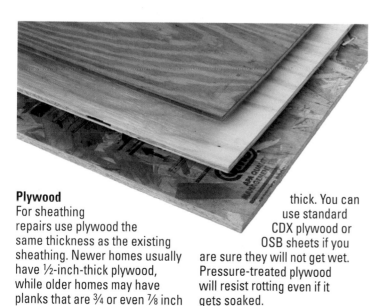

Plywood
For sheathing repairs use plywood the same thickness as the existing sheathing. Newer homes usually have ½-inch-thick plywood, while older homes may have planks that are ¾ or even ⅞ inch thick. You can use standard CDX plywood or OSB sheets if you are sure they will not get wet. Pressure-treated plywood will resist rotting even if it gets soaked.

WSU
Also called ice-guard membrane, waterproof shingle underlayment (WSU) stays waterproof even after nails have been driven through it. After removing the release paper, it sticks to the sheathing. There are various types, some with plastic coatings, some with mineral granules, and some with fiberglass reinforcement. It is common practice now to install a course of WSU along the lower edges of a roof, especially along eaves where ice dams could form. It is also sometimes used under valley flashing, where a roof meets a wall, and in other places where extra protection is desirable.

PREPARING THE SITE

A roofing job can generate a large amount of debris, especially if you need to tear off the existing roof. Protect your house, plantings, lawn, and driveway by covering the places where the junk will fall. You'll probably find that you can't cover the entire lawn area; fortunately it is possible to pick up most nails with a magnet. Do not cover a lawn with plastic sheeting for more than a few hours (especially if the sun is shining on it) or you could damage or kill the grass.

Secure the ladders (pages 22–24) and clear the way for safe walkways. To protect your lawn place sheets of plywood or planks in heavy foot-traffic areas. If you need a roll-off trash container, ask if it can be placed on your driveway without damaging the concrete or asphalt. Otherwise park it on the street or in an alley.

Cover up

Falling nails, granules, and other debris can damage the workings of an air-conditioner unit. Cover it with plastic sheeting and tape or tie the sheeting so it won't blow away. Cover nearby shrubs with a cloth drop cloth or old sheet. If you have a flowerbed that is in the drop zone, lean a piece of plywood over the bed or use stakes and a drop cloth to make a tent over delicate plants.

Create a stress-free work area.

If you will be tearing off, place a roll-off trash container as near as possible without damaging your yard or driveway. Make it as easy as possible to get up and down from the roof. Route power cords and air hoses so you can easily move them around on the roof.

A certain amount of mess is inevitable, so be prepared. Much of the debris can be removed from a lawn using a lawn rake. A nail magnet (page 26) makes quick work of picking up galvanized nails, though it will not work for aluminum or copper nails. A heavy-duty push broom is indispensable for cleaning the roof sheathing, driveway, and sidewalks.

Suspend tarp to protect house, catch debris

Cover air-conditioner

Roll-off trash container

Plywood to protect plantings

Plywood to protect lawn

Work surface

Organize the materials. Roofing is usually an uncomplicated job with few tools and materials to keep track of. But you don't want to have to wander around on the roof looking for things. Use a simple platform like the one shown to hold smaller items and tools.

Protect the shingles. If shingles will be stacked for more than a day, store them out of the sun to keep them from sticking together. Stack the bundles neatly on top of planks and cover with plastic sheeting to protect the paper wrapping from any rain.

SAFETY FIRST
Take it easy on your back

Whenever you continually lift heavy (or even medium-weight) objects, you are in danger of straining your back. Develop good habits early in the job; one wrong move could put you out of action for weeks. Whenever possible carry and lift with your back straight; lift from the knees, not the back. Carrying shingles under your arm will also strain your back.

To pick up a bundle of shingles, first slide it onto your thigh, as shown. Then, keeping your back straight, swing it onto your shoulder to carry the bundle.

WORKING SAFELY

Working on a roof can be safe if you consistently follow basic precautions.

In general never work in a place where you could possibly slide or fall off the roof; always have support for both feet and a way to stop yourself in case you start to slip.

Do not work on a steep roof (steeper than 8:12); leave that to the pros.

Stay clear of power lines.

Take the time to anchor ladders so there is no possibility that they will tilt over.

Avoid working after drinking alcohol or taking medications that make you drowsy.

Always have at least one helper who can assist you if you get into a tight spot.

If you hire a helper, make sure he or she is protected with medical insurance and worker's compensation insurance.

Stay alert for dangerous circumstances, such as loose shingles.

Treat a power nailer like a loaded gun. Keep it pointed away from yourself and others. Do not disable or attempt to circumvent the safety mechanism.

Use a ladder only if it is in good shape. Do not use one that has a broken rung, a missing or loose shoe, or a malfunctioning rung lock.

For the greatest protection against injuries, use a roof anchor attached to a body harness, as shown on page 25.

Wasps and yellow jackets often live in eaves and other areas of the roof. Don't let one sting cause you to fall. Don't panic; maintain a safe secure footing.

Using an extension ladder

1 Do not extend the ladder yet. Hold the ladder perpendicular to the wall with its feet out from the wall about one-fourth the height to which it will be raised. Have a helper brace the feet while you raise the ladder above your head, then walk toward the house, elevating the ladder with upraised arms as you go. Allow the ladder to rest against the house.

2 While the helper presses out to move the top of the ladder slightly away from the house, brace the bottom of the ladder with your foot and pull on the fly section's rope or push up on the fly section itself to raise it. Extend the fly section until it is slightly higher than you need it, then allow it to slide back down until both rung locks engage.

WHAT IF...
You are uncomfortable with heights?

The greatest measure of safety is achieved by using scaffolding rather than a ladder. Scaffolding can usually be rented by the week for a reasonable price. A scaffold that is 10 feet high or so can be erected by two people in 30 minutes to 1 hour. Some scaffolding has wheels so that you can move it without dismantling it.

A bonus: With a scaffold the ease and quality of your work will improve because you have a large, stable work area.

Ladder technique

Use standoff stabilizers to protect the gutters. When climbing a ladder keep your hips inside the side rails. Do not lean over to reach something several feet away; move the ladder. Do not climb higher than the third rung from the top. Do not step on a rung that is more than 1 foot above the point where the ladder is leaning.

To get onto a roof, climb the ladder until your feet are about level with the roofline. Hold both side rails firmly and step with your right foot onto the roof, keeping your left foot on the rung. Do not lean forward onto the top of the ladder. Move your left hand to the right side rail to hold the ladder as you step onto the roof with your left foot.

To get onto a ladder from the roof, grab the tops of both side rails with your hands. Swing your left foot onto the rung near its center. Once you achieve stability slide your left foot over slightly and swing your right foot onto the rung. Do not lean forward on the ladder at any time.

SAFETY FIRST
Anchor a ladder

Make sure a ladder is stable before you climb onto it. If the ground is not level, dig a quick hole (you can use a hammer) to lower one leg or place a plank under a leg to raise it. To ensure that the bottom won't kick out, drive stakes against both legs or drive a single stake and tie the ladder to it. You also may choose to tie the top of the ladder to an eyehook driven temporarily into the fascia.

STANLEY PRO TIP

Carrying shingles onto a roof

If you need to carry bundles of shingles onto a roof, ensure that the ladder is very stable. Anchor it at the bottom; tie it with a rope at the top. Carry the bundle on your shoulder, holding your back erect. The front of the bundle should go to the right or left of the side rail. Keep your hips inside the side rails and grab the rungs with one hand as you ascend.

Ladder secured to hook

Using roof jacks

1 Roof jacks provide a stable surface from which to work, increasing safety and making it easier to apply roofing. Ideally, locate a rafter below the sheathing. (You can usually feel sheathing nails, which are driven into rafters through the underlayment.) Attach a jack by driving two 16d nails (never roofing nails) into a rafter.

2 Slip whichever size board—usually a 2×8 or 2×10—will fit snugly into the jacks. The plank should overhang the jacks by about 6 inches on each side. Secure the plank to the jack as shown to prevent the jack from tipping over.

3 To remove a jack when you're done with it, tap up with a hammer to disengage the jack from the nails. To drive the nails in so they don't poke through the roofing, slip a flat pry bar under the shingle and over the nailhead and pound the nail down. Or, if the tab is flexible enough, lift it as you nail.

Roofing ladder

To extend your reach from ladder jacks, build a rough ladder out of 2×4s and 1×4s. Rest the ladder against the roof jack plank. Make sure that the ladder cannot slide under the plank.

Air hose fastener

Secure cords and pneumatic hoses so they will not slide off the roof, pulling an expensive saw or nailer with them. You can use a ladder clip like this one or simply tie cords to the ladder.

Using roof anchors

Shock absorber

1 Attach a roof anchor. Roof anchors can be installed easily and guarantee safety. They are often required by OSHA. Use deck screws (not gold-colored general-purpose screws) and be sure the fasteners penetrate a framing member, not just the sheathing.

2 Clip on the rope. Use heavy-duty braided polyester rope and approved hardware for clipping to the roof anchor. Make sure the rope cannot come loose. Ropes like the one shown have a built-in shock absorber to cushion a fall.

3 Strap on a body harness and clip on the rope. If you use a self-retracting lifeline, the rope will stay taut so you won't have excess rope to trip over as you work.

ROOF ANCHOR OPTIONS

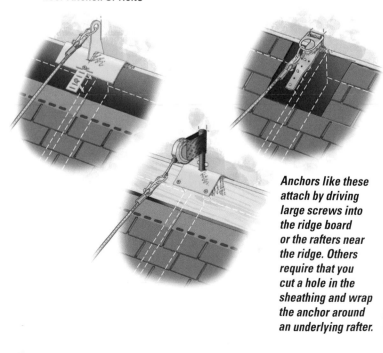

Anchors like these attach by driving large screws into the ridge board or the rafters near the ridge. Others require that you cut a hole in the sheathing and wrap the anchor around an underlying rafter.

Wear protective clothing

If you are working below others who are roofing or tearing off, wear a hard hat. Use eye protection when tearing off or driving nails. Roofers often wear gym shoes to help them keep from falling; a pair of rock-climbing boots is the ideal footwear. Long clothing will protect you from scrapes and the sun, but you may prefer short sleeves and shorts if it gets really hot. Invest in a high-quality pair of knee pads that won't chafe the back of your legs.

ROOFING TOOLS

If you have a basic set of carpentry tools, you won't need to buy many extra tools for a roofing job. Hand tools are not expensive, so it's usually a good idea to buy one even if you will only use it once. Roofing is usually done with a helper or two, so you may need to buy two or more of some tools.

Most often you will be using only a hammer, utility knife, chalkline, square, and **tape measure.** Keep these tools in a comfortable cloth or leather tool pouch.

Hand tools
Hand-nail roofing shingles with a **roofing hammer,** (sometimes called a hatchet) which has an adjustable gauge for quickly aligning shingles at the correct exposure. A standard 16- or 20-ounce **hammer** is often needed for sheathing repairs and general carpentry. Buy a hammer that feels comfortable in your hand. A **hammer stapler** makes quick work of attaching underlayment but is not suitable for shingles. A **flat pry bar** comes in handy for repair work and lifting up shingles.

A **margin trowel** is ideal for scooping roofing cement out of a bucket and applying it. Use a **caulking gun** to apply cement and caulk to small areas. Buy a caulking gun that stops dispensing when you release the trigger to prevent messy dribbles.

Use a **framing square** or a **layout square** as a cutting guide. A **chalkline** is indispensable for marking long, straight lines. You may need a **level** to determine roof pitch and to build small structures like a chimney cricket. Transfer angles with a **sliding bevel.** For cutting shingles use a **utility knife.** You may prefer one that retracts or one with a fixed blade. Have plenty of heavy-duty blades on hand. **Hooked blades** cut quickly through composition shingles and avoid damaging underlying surfaces as you cut. Use **tin snips** to cut flashings.

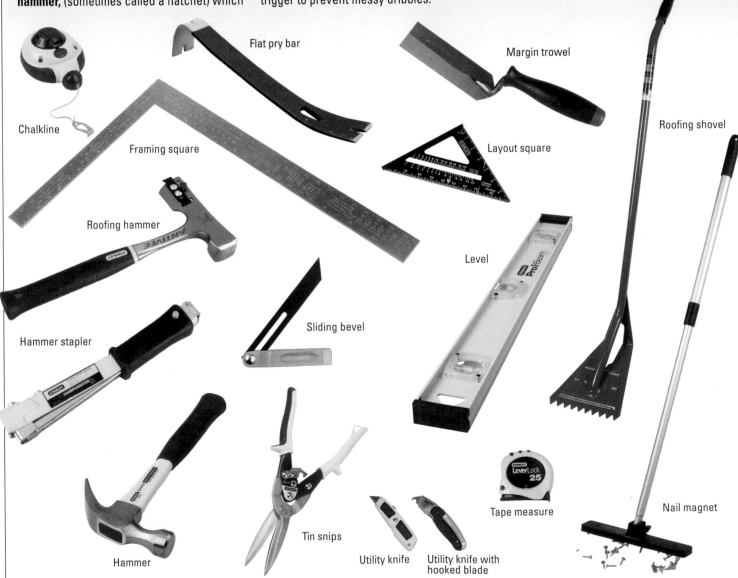

Flat pry bar

Margin trowel

Chalkline

Framing square

Layout square

Roofing shovel

Roofing hammer

Level

Hammer stapler

Sliding bevel

Tin snips

Utility knife

Utility knife with hooked blade

Tape measure

Nail magnet

Hammer

Tear-off and cleanup tools

When tearing off old roofing, a **roofing shovel** (also called a shingle ripper) both pries off the shingles and removes nails. Several types and sizes are available. Some roofers also like to use a standard pitchfork. You'll find a wide shovel handy for removing large amounts of rubbish; a narrow shovel is sometimes the best demolition tool in tight spots. For cleanup it pays to have a good **push broom, lawn rake,** and **nail magnet.**

Power tools

A power nailer makes the job go much faster. Be sure your nailer can drive nails suitable for the roofing you will be using. A **pneumatic nailer** requires a compressor and a long hose. A **cordless power nailer** needs no **compres**

For sheathing repairs and other carpentry work, use a **drill** with a **screwdriver bit** to quickly drive screws. An 18-volt cordless drill is convenient to use and has all the power you need. Use a **circular saw** for basic cutting and a **reciprocating saw** for cutting in tight spots.

SAFETY FIRST
GFCI-protected extension cord

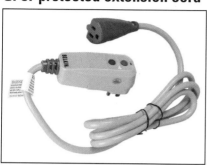

Use safe extension cords: If you are not already plugged into a GFCI-protected electrical receptacle, use a GFCI-protected extension cord. An extension cord with multiple outlets will keep you from having to unplug one tool in order to plug in another one. Some cords can retract or reel in to minimize dangling cords.

Circular saw

Drill with screwdriver bit

Caulking gun

Reciprocating saw

Compressor

Lawn rake

Pneumatic nailer

Push broom

Hose

INSTALLING ASPHALT SHINGLES

Asphalt shingles, also called composition shingles (they may be made largely of fiberglass), are the most common type of roofing for homes. They are inexpensive, come in a wide range of colors and profiles, are easy to install, and are suitable for a wide range of climates. (See page 8 for more background on this versatile material.)

This chapter shows how to install three-tab composition shingles, the most popular type. If you choose another kind, such as random-cutout or architectural (laminated) shingles, installation will be similar—it could be even simpler.

Be sure to follow manufacturer's recommendations printed on the bundle for nail positioning and shingle layout.

Nailing the shingles can be done by hand using a roofing hatchet, but working with any speed takes practice. (Years ago experienced roofers developed the technique of getting a nail ready between the two fingers of one hand while they pounded a nail—usually in two whacks—with the other hand.)

Today many pros and do-it-yourselfers prefer to apply roofing with a pneumatic nail gun and a compressor or a cordless power nailer (see page 27). You can rent a pneumatic or power nailer from a home center or a rental store. Be sure to specify that you will use the nailer for roofing so you will get the right kind of nailer. Buy the correct nails for your situation when you pick up the rental equipment.

Another major advantage of power nailers is that you can work with gloves on—hand-nailing requires at least one bare hand to hold the nails. Roofing is notoriously hard on hands; cold weather can make the job even more unpleasant. Gloves provide an added layer of protection, warmth, and a surer grip for handling bundles of shingles.

Asphalt shingles are inexpensive, come in a wide range of colors and profiles, and install easily.

CHAPTER PREVIEW

Preparing for the job
page 30

Roofing over existing shingles
page 32

Tearing off old shingles
page 36

Repairing sheathing
page 38

Working on steep roofs
Roofs like this require extra safety equipment such as a harness and safety rope. See page 25.

While you can learn to hand-nail shingles quickly, a pneumatic nailer dramatically speeds up the job. When used properly it is safer too: You won't hit your thumb.

Applying underlayment
page 40

Installing pre-shingle flashings
page 42

Installing three-tab shingles
page 44

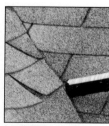

Installing valleys and chimney flashing
page 50

PREPARING FOR THE JOB

Start by ensuring that the roof structure—the sheathing and the rafters—is sound. Some springiness between rafters is not unusual, especially if the sheathing is ½-inch plywood. However if the roof feels bouncy when you step hard on a rafter or if the roof is obviously wavy, consult a carpenter; the framing may need to be strengthened. This can sometimes be done by adding supports in the attic between the ceiling joists and the rafters. In some cases each rafter may need to be strengthened by fastening another joist, called a "sister," to it.

Planning the job
Determine whether or not you need to tear off the old roof (see the Pro Tip opposite). Then plan how you will run the shingles. Decide how important it is to you for the cutouts in the shingles to line up accurately (see page 44). If you have a valley, decide whether you want an open metal, closed-cut, or woven style (see pages 50–52). Check for obstructions, such as dormers, that will complicate the layout (see page 46).

Keep an eye on the weather and plan accordingly. You should not shingle while rain is falling. Also avoid very hot and sunny days; not only is it uncomfortable, but you can damage the shingles by walking on them when they are very hot. It may make sense to start work just as the sun comes up, take a long midday break, and go back to work in the evening. Expect the job to take a day or two longer than you think it will.

Arranging for an inspection
Consult your local building department to get a permit before you start the job. Building codes are in place to protect your home. Your area may have conditions—high winds, for instance—that call for special materials and installation techniques. Building departments vary greatly in their procedures. Some simply require you to pay a fee and give assurances that you will install the right materials. With others, you need to schedule one or more inspections during the work. Be clear on points at which inspections must be done and don't cover up work that the inspector will want to see. It's rarely a good idea to argue with an inspector. Make it clear that you want to do the job right and that you will follow the inspector's recommendations.

You can get into trouble if you do the job without the proper permit. A roofing job is quite visible, and many municipalities have inspectors who will investigate when they see a nonpermitted job in progress (a roll-off trash container is a tipoff). If caught, you could be fined and even required to undo work you have done.

To make the best use of your time, gather the needed tools and materials in advance. Prepping the roof (sheathing repairs, flashing) can be as time-consuming as the roofing installation itself.

STANLEY PRO TIP: **Tear off or reroof?**

Tearing off an old roof (see pages 36–37) is difficult, time-consuming work. Professional roofers typically charge twice as much for a roofing job and tearing off as they do for a reroof (sometimes called a "layover").

When do you need to tear off? The short answer is: Whenever the inspector tells you to. The roof structure can support only so much weight. In general, if a roof has only one layer of asphalt shingles, it is okay to add a second. And in some cases you can add a third. Many factors are involved. Some shingles weigh more than others: 20-year shingles are the lightest, 40-year shingles weigh twice as much, and architectural shingles weigh even more. Also fiberglass-reinforced shingles weigh less than those made only of asphalt.

To find out how many layers your roof has, lift up the shingles at a rake edge. At the eaves' edge a single roof usually has two layers of roofing—the starter strip and the first course.

Another consideration: If the existing roofing shingles are curling, the new shingles will not be heavy enough to lie flat—so you probably need to tear off. (Heavy architectural shingles may lie flat; experiment by laying a few on the roof—see page 33—and waiting for a day or two.) If many of the old shingles are cracked and have missing pieces, the new shingles will follow the contours of the gaps, so it's probably time to tear off.

Planning for vents

Purchase your air vents ahead of time so you can install them as you roof. Buy vents to match the size and shape of the existing vents so they will fit easily.

If you will install a roof vent, it is best to wait until you have nearly finished the roofing. That way you can cut the hole, install the vent, and apply the ridge shingles at the same time.

The order of work

Peruse the following pages to familiarize yourself with the process. A typical job follows these steps:

■ The old roofing and flashings are torn off and removed. Or (for a reroof job) the hip shingles and some of the old flashings are removed and the roofing is patched as needed. At this point your home is vulnerable because the roof can leak.

■ For a tear-off job, the underlayment (roofing felt and WSU) should be installed immediately after tearing off to protect the house. For a reroof job use tarps to protect the ridge and the areas exposed by removing flashings.

■ If you need to build a cricket for the back of the chimney, this is the time.

■ Most of the flashings, including drip edges and valley flashings, must be installed before the shingles.

■ The starter strip and shingles are laid. Step flashings, vent flashings, and vents are installed along with the shingles.

■ Counterflashings at the chimney are installed, as well as any flashings that rest on top of the shingles.

ROOFING OVER EXISTING SHINGLES

If conditions are right (see page 31), new shingles laid over old shingles can be just as attractive and durable as shingles laid on bare sheathing.

Installation is easier than for a tear-off job because you can use the existing shingles as guides for laying the new ones. But you must take care to install the shingles correctly so they lie flat. And a good job involves installing new flashings rather than relying on the existing ones.

Reroof jobs are sometimes done without replacing flashings. However installing new flashings—including special drip-edge flashings made for reroofing—will ensure a tight seal and a long life. Some roofers install a layer of waterproof shingle underlayment (WSU) over the existing shingles at the eave end, as would be done for a roof laid on bare sheathing (see page 40). This provides added protection against ice dams.

Asphalt shingles can be laid over cedar shakes or shingles, a job best left to pros. Beveled wood pieces called "horsefeathers" must be laid along the thick edges of the shakes to make a fairly flat surface.

PRESTART CHECKLIST

☐ **TIME**
With a helper two days to flash and roof 700 square feet

☐ **TOOLS**
Power nailer or roofing hatchet, tape measure, roofing shovel or flat pry bar, hammer, drill, carpenter's square, tin snips, utility knife, chalkline, broom

☐ **SKILLS**
Marking, measuring, cutting, fastening

☐ **PREP**
Gather the materials, set up ladders or scaffolding, and prepare the yard below.

☐ **MATERIALS**
Roof cement, flashing, nails for flashing, perhaps a WSU sheet, shingles, nails long enough to penetrate sheathing

1 Remove the ridge caps. You may wait until the roofing is nearly complete to do this so the ridge will not be exposed while you work. Doing it now will make it easier to keep the job clean. Use a roofing shovel or flat pry bar to pry out and remove the ridge shingles. Remove all nails.

2 Remove air vents and pipe flashings by prying out or unscrewing the fasteners holding the fixture. If you damage shingles while doing this, repair the shingles (see next step). Reuse a vent or flashing only if it is like new; otherwise replace it with a new one that will fit the hole or pipe.

ALIGNING LAYOVER SHINGLES

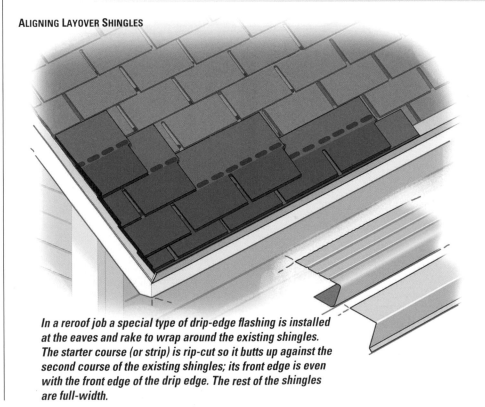

In a reroof job a special type of drip-edge flashing is installed at the eaves and rake to wrap around the existing shingles. The starter course (or strip) is rip-cut so it butts up against the second course of the existing shingles; its front edge is even with the front edge of the drip edge. The rest of the shingles are full-width.

3 Repair broken shingles. If a shingle has torn or cracked, glue the broken piece back in place using roofing cement. If the broken piece is lost, cut a piece to fit. The goal is to provide a reasonably flat surface for the shingles to lay over, with no gaps greater than ½ inch.

4 Sweep the roof. Brush away all broken shingle pieces, twigs, and any other debris that could become trapped under the new shingles that you install. Keep the roof clean as you work too.

STANLEY PRO TIP

Choosing shingles for a layover job

The thicker the shingle (top), the better it will hide any imperfections in the roofing below. It's a good idea to use at least 40-year shingles; architectural shingles are an even better choice.

5 At the eave and the rake, install U-shape drip-edge flashing made for reroof jobs. Install the eave piece first, then the rake piece over it. The two pieces should meet neatly at the corners. Drive nails at high points on the underlying roof—the bottoms of the shingles.

6 If you have an open valley, install new W-shape metal or vinyl valley flashing to fit directly over the old flashing. (See pages 50–51 for detailed instructions.) Attach it by driving nails into the outside edges only. Do not drive nails less than 6 inches from the center of the flashing.

WHAT IF...
You have a closed-cut or woven valley?

For a closed-cut (shown) or woven valley, first apply a roll of 36-inch-wide WSU. Work carefully to avoid any bubbles or creases (see page 41). Then install the new shingles in closed-cut or woven fashion (see pages 51–52).

7 Use a starter strip or cut pieces for a starter course (see pages 45–46). Rip-cut the starter strip or starter pieces so that they butt up against the second course of existing shingles and are even with the front edge of the existing roofing. Attach with nails along the top edge of the strip.

8 Rip-cut the shingles for the first course so they butt up against the third course of existing shingles and are even with the front edge of the starter course. Their tab slots should not line up with the tab slots of the starter course, if there are any. Nail the shingles just above the tab slots.

9 Butt the succeeding courses of shingles against the bottoms of existing shingles and apply them by driving nails above the tab slots. See page 47 for how to align the tab slots. Snap vertical control lines; there is no need to snap horizontal lines. Be sure the new tab slots do not align with the old ones.

STANLEY PRO TIP: **What to do if the old roof is not straight**

If the existing roof was installed poorly and has wavy horizontal lines, you can take out the waves by snapping a horizontal line ½ inch below the shingle bottoms of one course. Install a course along the snapped line, then install succeeding courses using a guide or a snapped line. (Shingles, especially if they are 40-year or architectural types, can span a gap of ½ inch.)

10 Once you have installed shingles just past a plumbing vent, install the flashing piece so it will lie on top of roofing at its bottom but be covered with roofing at its top. Depending on the width of the pipe, you may need to tear away a segment or two of the rubber boot. Apply roofing cement, slide the flashing over the pipe, and push so it lies flat on the roof. (See page 48 for details.)

11 Install air vents in a similar manner. For both plumbing-vent flashing and air vents, you'll need to cut the shingle above to go around the flashing and then install the shingle.

12 Where you meet a chimney or side wall, install step flashing (see pages 52–53). Apply a shingle, then a piece of flashing, then a shingle, and so on, so that each piece of flashing rests on top of the lower course and is covered by the upper course. You'll need to pry the siding outward to slip in the flashing; in some cases you'll have to remove the siding.

13 Protect the step flashing with counterflashing. On a chimney use a grinder to cut an indentation into the mortar. Cut and bend the counterflashing to fit snugly into the cut mortar and to cover at least 3 inches of the step flashing. Apply mortar with a caulking gun (inset) and set the flashing into the mortar.

14 Install roofing on both sides of a ridge and cut them so they butt closely together but do not overlap. Cut shingles into ridgecaps. Snap lines on either side and install the caps (see pages 48–49).

15 At the rake snap a line directly above the edge of the existing shingles. Cut with a utility knife; you may want to use a straightedge. You may find it easier if you first cut from below using the existing shingles as a cutting guide.

TEARING OFF OLD SHINGLES

Stripping asphalt shingles from a roof fairly quickly is not as difficult as you may expect—the hard part is the waste removal. Gathering and getting off old shingles is a dirty, tiring job. It is well worth planning your project carefully.

Find a disposal company that will haul away old roofing. Call around for the best price. If you tell the salesperson how large the roof is, he or she should be able to accurately estimate the size trash container you will need. If you need two containers, have them delivered the same day so your house does not sit partially unprotected overnight.

It's easiest to shovel and sweep downward, so place the trash container beneath the largest portion of the roof if possible. Or you can lay a large tarp on the ground and shovel trash onto it. However you will have to pick up the debris and transport it to the trash container in wheelbarrows. (See page 20 for an example of a site prepared for tear-off.)

1 Start the tear-off at the ridge. Use a roofing shovel (also known as a shingle ripper) or a flat pry bar to pry up and remove the ridgecaps.

2 Working from the top down, slip a roofing shovel under the shingles, push until you encounter a nail, and pry up. Take it easy here: Medium pressure is better than pushing hard.

PRESTART CHECKLIST

☐ **TIME**
Working with a helper plan for most of a day to tear shingles and flashing off a 700-square-foot roof, transport it to a trash bin, and clean up the yard.

☐ **TOOLS**
Roofing shovel or flat pry bar, wide and narrow shovels, pitchfork, hammer, wheelbarrow, broom, nail magnet, tin snips, utility knife

☐ **SKILLS**
Working safely on heights

☐ **PREP**
Arrange for placing the trash bin and protect the lawn and plantings with tarps.

☐ **MATERIALS**
Tarps, plywood

TRASH BIN ARRANGEMENTS

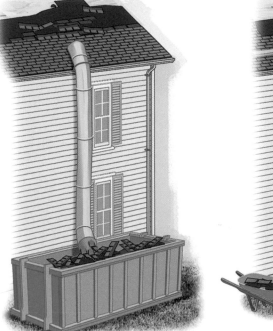

If you can get the container close enough, rent a chute. If you can strip only part of the roof directly into the bin from a chute, save that part for last. Open the trash container's gate and load with a wheelbarrow first, then close the gate and fill the rest of the bin from the roof.

3 Use the shovel as both a prying tool and a shovel to move the debris. If a trash bin or tarp is below, carefully shovel directly into it. Otherwise stop before the pile gets out of control, pick up the garbage with gloved hands or a large shovel, and carry it away.

4 Use the shovel or a pry bar to pry out all the nails. Do not pound the nails in. Watch for nails embedded sideways in the sheathing or wedged in joints.

5 Remove all vents and pipe flashings. Work carefully when you get close to a pipe, especially if it is plastic. Pry up the nails holding a pipe flashing or a vent and lift it out. Take care not to spill debris down the hole and into the attic.

6 Remove valley and drip-edge flashings. It may be tempting to leave the old flashings in place, but these should be removed so you can install new, reliable flashings along with the new shingles. Also remove the step flashings.

There is one exception: You may choose to retain counterflashings (see page 53). Counterflashings can often be removed in good enough shape that you can use them as templates for cutting new pieces.

7 Use a push broom to sweep away all debris. Even small pieces of shingles and twigs will create bumps in the underlayment and shingles, so be diligent about cleaning. Check for any overlooked nails by dragging the back of the broom across the sheathing.

REPAIRING SHEATHING

Once the old roof has been torn off, repair any damaged sections of sheathing. Inspect the plywood and planks; repairs are usually relatively easy and quick.

A roof does not have to be as firm as a floor, but it should be strong enough to hold the roofing without sagging. If the roof has dips that can be spotted from the ground, be sure to make repairs in those areas.

If the edge along an eave is rotted or otherwise damaged, be sure to inspect the fascia board and rafter ends as well. This is a common location for rot. Replace any damaged fascia boards (see pages 176–177). If rafter ends are rotted 2 inches deep or less, you may be able to solve the problem by applying liquid wood hardener. Or cut away the damaged area and install a "sister" piece alongside the rafter. Then cover the rafters with fascia and soffit boards. Repair sheathing with plywood that is the same thickness as the existing sheathing if possible. Pressure-treated plywood is affordable and will prevent rot.

PRESTART CHECKLIST

☐ **TIME**
Once you have the materials, less than an hour for most sheathing repairs

☐ **TOOLS**
Tape measure, circular saw, framing square, layout square, chalkline, drill, hammer, screwdriver

☐ **SKILLS**
Basic measuring and cutting

☐ **PREP**
Remove shingles, flashings, and nails

☐ **MATERIALS**
½-inch or ¾-inch plywood or OSB (oriented strand board) to match the existing sheathing, 2×6 boards, 16d nails or 3-inch deck screws, 8d nails or 2-inch deck screws, underlayment

1 Check for damage. Look for places where the sheathing is rotted or discolored from water damage. Poke with a screwdriver; if it goes in easily, the wood is rotted. You can also inspect from inside the attic. Shine a flashlight at the sheathing and rafters and poke with a screwdriver.

2 Remove the damaged area. Use a chalkline or a pencil and framing square to mark a rectangle around the damaged area that spans from the inside of a joist to the inside of another joist. (Do not attempt to cut along the center of the joists.) Use a circular saw to cut out the rectangle.

WHAT IF...
The sheathing is extra-thick?

If you have an older home with sheathing that is ⅞ inch thick or thicker, patching with ½- or ¾-inch-thick material will leave an undesirable indentation. To smooth things out install nailers so they are slightly raised above the tops of the joists. Hold a scrap of patching plywood on top of the nailer and drive a 3-inch deck screw or 16d nail so that when the patch is inserted, it is flush with the adjoining sheathing.

3 Pull out the damaged plywood and inspect the rafters below. If they are slightly rotted, install long sister rafters, made of boards the same width as the rafters, alongside them instead of the nailers shown in the next step. Attach the sisters from inside the attic. If the damage is extensive, call a carpenter for advice.

4 Attach pieces of 2×6 alongside the insides of the rafters to provide a nailing surface for a plywood patch. Attach the nailers with 16d nails or 3-inch screws.

5 Cut a patch to fit snugly (but not so tightly that you have to pound it into place). Set it in place and drive 8d nails or 2-inch screws into the rafters and nailers.

6 Cover the patch with underlayment. The patch and the surrounding sheathing should look and feel fairly level.

APPLYING UNDERLAYMENT

Before applying roofing cover the sheathing with roofing felt, also often called "tar paper." Do not use felt as a temporary protection against rain: If it gets wet it will wrinkle, making it harder to shingle. If you need to temporarily protect a roof, cover it with plastic sheeting or a tarp.

Most local codes call for using 30-pound felt; see page 19 for more information. Some roofers prefer to attach felt underlayment with 1-inch roofing nails or special nails with plastic washers, but most codes allow staples, which are easier to drive. For the lower portion of the roof—especially the part that overhangs the eaves and is susceptible to ice dams—it is a good idea to apply self-stick waterproof shingle underlayment (WSU), also called ice guard.

Underlayment, flashings, and shingles all work together and must be installed in the correct order. Read pages 40–53 to help plan the total job.

If you lay the felt perfectly straight, you can use its lines (instead of horizontal chalklines) to align the shingles.

PRESTART CHECKLIST

☐ **TIME**
Working with a helper, several hours to install drip edge, WSU, and roofing felt on a medium-sized roof

☐ **TOOLS**
Tin snips, hammer, hammer stapler, utility knife, tape measure, chalkline

☐ **SKILLS**
Basic measuring, careful laying out

☐ **PREP**
Sweep the sheathing clean of all debris and make sure there are no nails or splinters poking up.

☐ **MATERIALS**
Drip edge, WSU, roofing felt, staples or roofing nails

1 Apply drip edge to the eave. Cut drip edge flashing at an angle at the corner, press it lightly against the eave end (not too hard or you will misshape it), and drive a nail near the end. Use a chalkline or align it by eye to make sure it is straight and drive roofing nails every foot or so to fasten it to the sheathing.

2 Where drip-edge pieces meet, overlap them by at least 2 inches. Where the drip edge meets a valley or a hip, cut the pieces as shown, with overlapping tabs. Press the tabs firmly to make crisp corners with no gaps and attach with roofing nails.

STANLEY PRO TIP

Double-task it

When the weather promises to stay dry, many roofers prefer to install underlayment as they go. Apply one or two courses of WSU or felt, install the shingles, then apply more felt when you come within 6 inches of the top edge.

Prepping a hip roof

Where you meet a hip, apply felt up to the hip and cut the pieces so they fit snugly. Then apply a vertical course of felt along the hip that overlaps on each side.

3 Snap a chalkline to help you align the WSU or felt. The WSU should overhang the drip edge by ½ inch, so snap a line that is 35½ inches above the drip edge. Check at several points to make sure the overhang is consistent; it does not have to be perfect, but you may need to realign the drip edge.

4 Using the chalkline as a guide, roll out about 12 feet of WSU smooth and free of creases and bubbles. Often you can reroll it, then unroll it while peeling off the paper backing. On a steep roof (shown), you can adhere the bottom half first, then pull off the backing from above. Avoid creases and stay aligned with the chalkline. Press down to tightly seal the WSU.

5 No matter which valley method you use (see the illustrations on page 42–43, and pages 50–52), for extra protection apply WSU at a valley. Snap chalklines on both sides for guides. Roll out and smooth the WSU and drive a few nails on one side to hold it temporarily. Fold over the other side and peel off the paper backing. Press into place, remove the nails, and peel off the paper on the other side.

6 Overlap felt courses at least 4 inches. Snap a chalkline 32 inches above the top edge of the WSU or use the lines on the felt as guides. If you use the lines as guides for installing shingles, measure up from the drip edge to confirm that you stay parallel. Roll out the felt, eliminating creases or bubbles, and drive at least three staples every foot.

7 Apply felt right up to the ridge or to no more than 4 inches below it. (Rather than cutting the felt horizontally to fit, overlap it by more than 4 inches.) Apply felt on the ridge so it overlaps at least 8 inches on each side. Eliminate creases and bubbles.

8 Where the roof meets a wall, lap the felt up 4 inches if possible. Pry away the siding and slip the felt under the siding. In some situations you may have to temporarily remove the siding and replace it after installing the underlayment, shingles, and flashing (see Step 12, page 35).

INSTALLING PRE-SHINGLE FLASHINGS

If you will install an open metal valley, the valley flashing must be installed after the underlayment and before the shingles; follow the instructions here. If you will be installing a woven or closed-cut valley, there is no need for valley flashing. However, a strip of WSU (page 41) is highly recommended.

Roofers sometimes make their own valley flashings out of sheet metal, but you are better off buying ready-made valley flashing. The type with a center spine (or ridge) works best because it channels water more efficiently and permits expansion and contraction of the metal. Valley flashing with nailing clips prevents puncturing the flashing, but you can also nail the flashing directly if you do so carefully.

The drip edge along the rake is also installed at this time. In most cases you will use the same type of drip edge as you used for the eave (page 40).

PRESTART CHECKLIST

☐ **TIME**
1 to 2 hours to cut and install flashings for a valley and rake ends

☐ **TOOLS**
Tin snips, tape measure, hammer, chalkline

☐ **SKILLS**
Measuring and cutting metal, driving nails

☐ **PREP**
Apply the underlayment, preferably with a strip of WSU along the valley.

☐ **MATERIALS**
Valley flashing, roofing nails

Valley flashing

1 Use tin snips to carefully cut the flashing in a V-shape so it slightly extends beyond the drip edge at the eaves. If you saved the old valley flashing, use it as a template.

2 Set the first piece of valley flashing in place, check its alignment, and make sure both sides lie flat on the roof. Drive nails next to the flashing so the nailheads capture the flashing but do not poke holes in it. (If your flashing has nailing clips, drive nails through the clips every foot or so on each side.)

OPEN METAL VALLEY

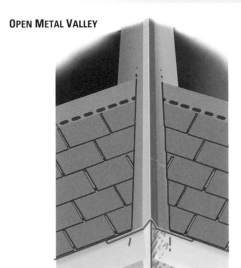

An open metal valley starts with a strip of metal valley flashing. Shingles lap over the flashing. In some installations they are run at a slight angle, so the bottom flashing exposure is wider than the top. Roofing cement (not nails) secures the shingles to the flashing.

WOVEN VALLEY

A woven (or closed) valley has no metal flashing. Instead shingles from each side overlap each other in an alternating pattern. A roll of WSU is usually used for the underlayment. The shingles for each side of the roof must be installed at the same time so you can weave them. No nails can be driven within 6 inches of the valley center.

Add drip edge along rake

3 Overlap valley flashing pieces by at least 8 inches. Align the flashings to make sure succeeding pieces form a straight line. To align them exactly stretch a mason's line or chalkline from the ridge of the roof to the eaves along the flashing center spine.

4 Where a valley meets a ridge, bend the flashing over so it laps onto the other side by at least 3 inches. You will need to cut the spine first. You may choose to apply a bead of roofing cement along the side of the flashing at this time; applying it later (see page 51) takes a bit more time but is less messy.

Along the rake end install drip edge on top of the underlayment. Cut the drip edge at a slight angle and make sure it neatly abuts the eave's drip edge. Nail it in place with 6d galvanized nails.

CLOSED-CUT VALLEY

On top of a sheet of WSU underlayment, install the shingles on one side so they lap over the valley; then overlap them, working from the other side. Using a protective sheet of metal, cut the top layer of shingles (see page 51). Drive no nails within 6 inches of the valley center.

STANLEY PRO TIP

Fasten them right

For most composition shingles use galvanized roofing nails. Roofing staples are also effective. The nails should be long enough to poke through the sheathing when driven into the roofing and underlayment. At the peak you will need longer nails because you will drive through two layers of roofing. (See page 19 for a description of various nails.)

Set the power nailer or practice hand-nailing to achieve the right nail depth: The head should be driven just flush with the roofing surface. Driving a head so that it is indented into the shingle will actually weaken the connection.

Planning for ventilation

If your attic gets very hot in the summer or does not get very cold in the winter (e.g., snow melts faster on your roof than on your neighbor's), you probably need to install roof ventilation. See pages 96–101 for various options. If you choose to install a ridge vent or roof vents, do so before you apply the shingles.

INSTALLING THREE-TAB SHINGLES

The three-tab asphalt shingle, also called a composition or fiberglass shingle (see page 8), is the most common type of shingle. Other composition shingles, such as architectural and random cutouts, are installed using most of the same techniques; check with your roofing dealer to learn about any installation differences.

Three-tab shingles are usually 36 inches long; each tab is 12 inches. They are designed to be installed with a 5-inch reveal. Some roofers install shingles so the cutout lines describe a slight angle as you look from the bottom to the top of the roof. However most people prefer the cutout lines to be aligned so they make straight vertical lines.

This section shows how to install shingles using the racking method shown on this page. On page 45 are two other layout methods. Each has its advantages.

A pneumatic nail gun makes quick work of fastening shingles. You can install shingles by hand using a roofing hatchet, but the work will proceed more slowly.

PRESTART CHECKLIST

☐ **TIME**
With one or two helpers, about 2 days to shingle a 1,500-square-foot roof

☐ **TOOLS**
Nail gun, tape measure, roofing hatchet, framing square, chalkline, pry bar, utility knife, straightedge, caulking gun, tin snips

☐ **SKILLS**
Measuring, laying out a job, driving nails, cutting with a knife

☐ **PREP**
Install underlayment, drip edge, and valley flashing as needed (pages 40–43).

☐ **MATERIALS**
Shingles, roofing nails long enough to fully penetrate the sheathing, roofing cement, flashings

1 Load the roof. If possible have the shingles delivered via a boom directly onto the roof. If the slope is shallow so there's no danger that the shingles will slide off, scatter the shingles on the roof so they will be in easy reach. Otherwise stack them near the ridge in a way that prevents them from sliding or on a roof-jack platform (shown).

RACKING LAYOUT

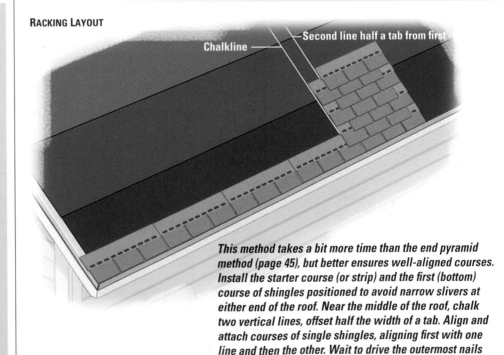

Chalkline — Second line half a tab from first

This method takes a bit more time than the end pyramid method (page 45), but better ensures well-aligned courses. Install the starter course (or strip) and the first (bottom) course of shingles positioned to avoid narrow slivers at either end of the roof. Near the middle of the roof, chalk two vertical lines, offset half the width of a tab. Align and attach courses of single shingles, aligning first with one line and then the other. Wait to drive the outermost nails on each side, so you can later slip in shingles.

2 Snap horizontal chalklines to help you keep the courses straight. First snap a line for the top of the starter course, whose bottom will be flush with the WSU or felt underlayment (which overhangs the drip edge by ½ inch). Then snap lines for every course or every other course. Assuming that the shingles have a 5-inch reveal, snap these lines in 5-inch increments, starting at the bottom of the underlayment. You may choose to snap lines for every course, every other course, or every third course.

3 Install a continuous starter strip (next page) or full-sized shingles, which are simply turned down-side up. Often, however, a starter course is made of cut shingles. Place the shingle upside down on a sheet of plywood and use a straightedge to cut it 7 inches wide; you will use the portion with no tabs.

PYRAMID LAYOUT METHOD, STARTING AT THE END OF THE ROOF

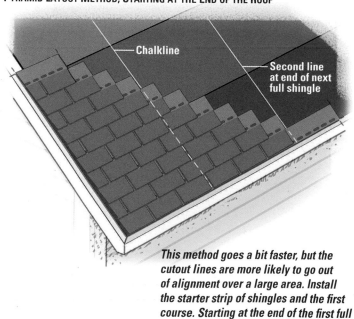

Chalkline

Second line at end of next full shingle

This method goes a bit faster, but the cutout lines are more likely to go out of alignment over a large area. Install the starter strip of shingles and the first course. Starting at the end of the first full shingle, chalk vertical lines at the end of each shingle.

PYRAMID LAYOUT METHOD, STARTING IN THE MIDDLE OF THE ROOF

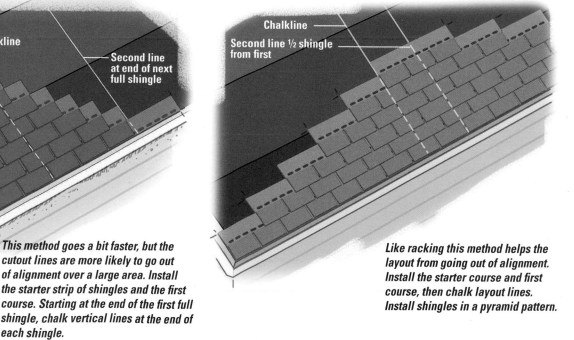

Chalkline

Second line ½ shingle from first

Like racking this method helps the layout from going out of alignment. Install the starter course and first course, then chalk layout lines. Install shingles in a pyramid pattern.

4 Starting at one end, place the starter shingles down-side up so the self-seal strip is near the bottom. The top should be aligned with the chalkline and the bottom should be flush with the bottom of the underlayment.

5 Attach each starter shingle by driving three nails along its top edge. Fastening along the top edge assures that nailheads will not be exposed.

6 To avoid ending up with a narrow strip of tab along one of the rakes, lay out a full course of shingles and adjust their position as needed.

STANLEY PRO TIP: **Speed the job**

Roofing hammers have an exposure gauge to speed the positioning of shingles. The pin hooks the course below; the new shingle rests on hammer head.

Precut starter strips (shown) or starter rolls save you the trouble of cutting a standard shingle laterally.

WHAT IF...
You must shingle around a dormer?

To roof around a dormer or other obstruction, install shingles all the way up and run at least one course past the obstruction. The bottom of these courses must be nailed higher than usual so you can slip shingles under them later. Now you can snap a new bond line to align the shingles on the other side.

7 To attach a shingle align it with the layout line and drive nails ½ inch above the cutout slots (including the half slots at each side). Drive a nail at one end first, then drive the others. If you are using a power nailer, drive nails by squeezing the trigger and bouncing the nailer's tip onto the shingle.

8 For a racking or midroof pyramid layout method (see pages 44–45), snap two vertical lines (called bond lines) near the center of the roof, the appropriate distance apart. Check them with a framing square or measure so the lines are parallel with the rake ends. It's better to use the factory edges of a half-sheet of plywood as a guide.

9 Install four or five courses of shingles along the bond lines in an alternating pattern as shown. Take care that the shingles are correctly aligned with consistent reveals. Later you will need to lift up the outermost ends of the shingles on each side in order to slip in a shingle, so don't drive the outermost nails now.

10 Starting at the racked shingles, fill in the courses. Align the shingles with the horizontal lines and nail them in place. Note: In areas with high winds, it is common to drive two nails above each cutout line.

11 Shingles often have small cuts on the top and sides that can be used as guides for horizontal and vertical alignment. Use these whenever there is no layout line. Also roofing hatchets have adjustable guides as do some roofing nailers.

12 To easily check your work or if you find the guide on the nailer awkward to use, make a simple plywood jig like the one shown as a guide for the 5-inch reveal.

13 If the roof is steep enough that you could slide off, install roof jacks and planks to keep you stable and safe. A scrap of roofing laid upside down beneath the heel of the jack will keep it from denting the shingles. (See page 24 for more about how to install roof jacks.)

14 When you encounter a plumbing vent pipe, shingle up to it so the flashing will rest on a row of shingles below the pipe. You may need to cut out part of the rubber flange so it fits over the pipe. Apply roofing cement (a caulk tube is usually the neatest and easiest method) where it will rest on top of shingles.

15 Slip the flashing over the pipe and press it in place. Drive nails around the perimeter as recommended by the manufacturer.

WHAT IF...
Hips meet at a ridge?

You may have to improvise to handle awkward areas. Just be sure that water will not seep in between shingles as it runs downward. Where two hips meet a ridge, cut a triangular piece to cover the joint. Cover any exposed nailheads with dabs of roofing cement. Then apply ridgecaps.

WHERE A RIDGE MEETS A ROOF

Winged WSU is applied first

WSU covers both and is in turn covered by the next course of shingles

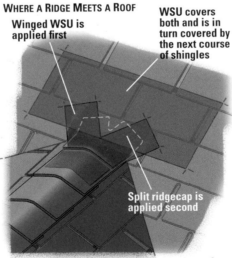

Split ridgecap is applied second

If you have a hip that runs into the main roof, cover the area with WSU when you are installing the sheathing; cut the WSU so it lies flat at all points. Then cover the resulting V-shape notch with another piece of WSU. When you install the shingles, leave one shingle unnailed so you can later slip a ridgecap under it.

Cutting rake ends as you go

Many professional roofers cut the rake-end shingles as they go rather than making an arduous chalkline cut. Hold each piece in place and mark it for cutting by nicking its top or bottom. Flip it over and cut, using a square as a guide. Every few courses check that the line is straight and overhanging the rake by ½ inch.

16 Roof around the vent. Cut the upper shingles so they fit snugly but do not ride up on the flashing's raised portion; the shingles should lie flat at all points. Where shingles overlap the flashing, attach them with roofing cement rather than nails. Cover any exposed nailheads with dabs of roofing cement.

17 Apply flashing at a wall. Where a wall is perpendicular to the roofing (shown), slip pieces of step flashing under the siding. Apply a flashing piece, then a shingle, then flashing, as you would apply step flashing for a chimney (see page 53). If the roof meets a wall that is parallel to the shingles, roof up to the wall, then slip a long continuous piece of flashing under the siding and on top of the shingles.

18 When you reach a peak or hip, shingle all the way up the first side (until the reveal portion of the shingles is within 4 inches of the peak) and cut the shingles just below the ridge. Shingle the other side and allow these pieces to overlap the ridge by no more than 4 inches.

19 To cut ridgecaps turn shingles upside down and cut off single tabs. Angle the cuts slightly so the nonreveal portions will not be visible when the caps are installed. Make a cut on the back side, then bend and break the shingle. Using a 5-inch reveal, estimate the number of caps needed. Prepare the ridge by snapping chalklines 6 inches on each side.

20 Install ridgecaps along the lines, leaving a 5-inch reveal. Drive the nails about 1½ inches from the sides and just below the self-sealing strip. Shingle to the middle of the ridge, then start from the other end. Where the ridgecaps meet install a 5-inch-wide strip. Cover nailheads with dabs of roofing cement.

21 Where the shingles overhang a rake, snap a chalkline, then use a straightedge and a knife equipped with a hook blade to cut the line. This is slow work and you may need to change blades several times.

INSTALLING VALLEYS AND CHIMNEY FLASHING

Valleys are notorious for developing leaks. In downpours torrents from two planes of the roof meet. Often they are dammed by debris. These factors can cause water to go under nearby shingles, resulting in leaks.

Pages 50–53 show you three ways to roof valleys: open metal, closed-cut, and woven. All three work well, but check which is preferred by your local building department. Whichever method you choose: Do not drive nails within 6 inches or so of the valley center or you will provide an unwanted pathway for water.

A strip of WSU provides extra protection and is an essential component of woven and closed-cut valleys. It is also a good idea for an open metal valley. See pages 40–41 for applying the WSU to a valley.

Chimney flashing (pages 52–53) is fairly complicated. If your chimney did not leak before and you can use the old flashing pieces as templates for the new, you should have no problems. However if you have no templates, you may want to call in a professional roofer.

PRESTART CHECKLIST

☐ **TIME**
Working with a helper, several hours to roof a typical valley

☐ **TOOLS**
Nail gun, tape measure, roofer's hatchet, chalkline, flat pry bar, straightedge, caulk gun, utility knife, tin snips

☐ **SKILLS**
Measuring, laying out, cutting with a knife

☐ **PREP**
Install WSU, drip-edge flashing, and valley flashing as needed (pages 40–43).

☐ **MATERIALS**
Composition shingles, roofing nails, roofing cement, flashing

Open metal valley

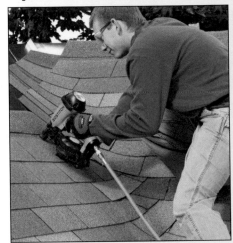

1 With underlayment and flashing installed (see pages 40–43), apply shingles up to one side of the flashing. Do not drive nails into the flashing. Then install shingles on the other side. Again do not drive nails through flashing. You'll have to overlap shingles as you go, much like weaving (see page 52).

2 Some roofers cut the shingles parallel to the flashing's center ridge. Others start with a 3-inch-wide gap at the top and widen the gap by ⅛ inch per running foot as it runs downward. Check with your inspector to see which method is preferred in your area. Snap chalklines for the cuts.

STANLEY PRO TIP: **Applying cement first**

Some roofers prefer to apply roofing cement to the flashing using a trowel rather than a caulking gun before they install the shingles. You can also apply cement between the shingles as you go using a trowel or a caulking gun. Be aware, however, that this method can get messy.

3 Place a piece of sheet metal under the shingles to make sure you will not damage the flashing. Use a utility knife with a hook blade to cut the shingles along the chalkline. You may find it helpful to use a straightedge as a guide.

4 Snipping off the corners of adjacent shingles (roofers call it dubbing) adds a measure of protection against water being channeled under shingles. Lift up shingles and use a hook blade to cut all the pointed unexposed ends. Make each cut about 2 inches from the point.

5 Caulk twice between shingles and flashing. Using roofing cement in a caulk tube, insert the tube's tip all the way under the shingles and run a continuous bead. Then hold the nozzle 2 inches back and apply a second bead nearer the edge.

6 Lift up each top shingle and apply roofing cement to adhere the shingles to each other. This is important both to seal out water and to attach the shingles because there are no nails.

Closed-cut valley

1 Roof one side of the valley, running the shingles across it. Stop nailing 6 inches from the center. Lay one- and two-tab shingles as you near the valley so full-size shingles will run across the valley. Shingle the other side of the valley the same way. Snap a chalkline 2 to 3 inches past the valley center on the top layer of shingles.

2 Cut the top layer of shingles along the chalkline. Slip a piece of sheet metal flashing under the top layer of shingles to protect the bottom layer in the valley while you cut the shingles with a hook blade.

3 Dub-cut the top-layer shingles (see Step 4 above). Apply two beads of roofing cement to attach the top-layer shingles to the bottom-layer shingles. Also apply cement to attach the top-layer shingles to each other (Steps 5 and 6 above).

Flashing around a chimney

1 Cut and bend the bottom flashing piece as shown. The flashing should be about 5 inches tall (against the chimney) and 5 inches wide (where it rests on the roof in front). The front top should wrap around the chimney an inch or so on each side.

2 Install roofing so the exposed portion runs at least up to the chimney. Apply roofing cement to the back and bottom of the flashing, press it into place, and tap its sides to wrap them around the chimney. Drive nails at the corners.

3 Buy ready-made step flashing pieces or cut and bend them yourself. Cut and bend the top front of the first step flashing piece so the bend will wrap around the plumb line of the chimney.

Weaving a valley

1 All woven pieces must be full-size shingles that lap onto the other side of the valley by at least 1½ tabs. The two sides of the valley must be shingled at the same time: Shingle a course on one side, then the other.

2 Attach the subsequent courses. Continue working on alternate sides to weave shingles across the valley. Do not drive nails within 6 inches of the valley center.

3 Use single- or double-tabbed shingles as needed. Every shingle that crosses the valley should be full-size and should lap the valley by at least 8 inches. To achieve this you will need to cut and attach single- or double-tabbed shingles just to the left or right of the overlapping shingles.

4 Install the first step flashing piece. Test the fit, then apply roofing cement to the back of the step flashing piece. Press it into place and drive nails near the bottom edge. Cover the nailheads with roofing cement.

5 Install roofing to cover the first step flashing piece. Apply roofing cement to the back of the next flashing piece and press it against the chimney so its front edge just covers the self-seal strip. Use roofing cement to cover the part that rests on the roof. Install the next shingle, the next flashing piece, and so on.

6 Counterflashing slips into grooves cut in the mortar joints above and runs over the step flashing and base flashing. If grooves have not already been cut in the mortar, use a grinder to make them (see page 35). Bend the counterflashing to fit into the grooves and run along the roofline; it should lap over the flashing by at least 3 inches at all points. Seal the mortar joints with silicone caulk.

WHAT IF...
You need to build a cricket?

If your cricket is damaged or missing, build one from 2× lumber and plywood or OSB (oriented-strand board). Cut 2× to fit against the chimney and create a peaked surface that extends to either side of the chimney. Measure for the length of the ridge board. Cut plywood or OSB to fit.

7 At the top and behind the chimney, run shingles over the cricket as you would a roof ridge. Cut flashing to fit; it will have a V-shape notch at the top. Install the flashing with nails and roofing cement.

8 Counterflash the top of the cricket. The counterflashing piece covering the cricket flashing has tabs that lap onto the flashing on both sides. Cover all exposed nailheads on the chimney flashing with dabs of roofing cement.

INSTALLING OTHER ROOFING

A roof goes a long way toward defining the look of a house, so it's not surprising to find a variety of great-looking and durable roofing products. (See pages 8–11 for a closer look at the range of options.) While asphalt shingles are affordable and appropriate for most any climate, the roofing types shown in this chapter offer a wider range of style, color, and durability. Some will last for 50 years or more.

Before installing a roofing product other than asphalt shingles, consult with a local supplier, your building department, or a local roofing professional. Make sure that

the product you choose is suitable for your climate and for the slope of your roof. Some types of roofing, such as slate, tar-and-gravel, and heavy clay tiles, are best installed by professionals. However many newer products, such as cement tiles, metal roofing, modified bitumen, EPDM (or rubber) roofing, and wood shakes, are within the reach of a do-it-yourselfer.

Whatever the roofing material the essential installation principles remain the same. However be sure you understand how all the components of your chosen material fit together. There may be special pieces for ridges, hips, and rake ends.

Fasteners and flashings may be material-specific as well.

Preparing for these roofs is often similar to preparation for a composition shingle roof. In most cases the sheathing should be cleared of old roofing and swept clean. Then apply WSU and/or roofing felt underlayment. In some cases new roofing can be installed over existing composition shingles.

Lay out the roof for cedar shakes, faux tiles, and concrete tiles as you would for composition shingles. For vertical metal roofing and flat roofing sheets (modified bitumen or EPDM), the layout is simpler.

CHAPTER PREVIEW

Whatever the roofing material the essential installation principles are the same.

Cedar shakes
page 56

Vertical metal roofing
page 62

Faux tiles
page 66

Tile roofs
page 68

Batten logic
Each cement tile has a lip that hangs on a cedar batten. The battens are spaced to allow some moisture to run down the underlayment.

Cement roofing tiles overlap each other and are nailed in place like other types of shingles. However they require support battens and special flashing—not to mention a strong back to heft them onto the roof. The payback is a high-quality, long-lasting roof.

Modified-bitumen roofing
page 74

Roll roofing
page 80

CEDAR SHAKES

Wood shingles—which are relatively smooth—are now more commonly installed as siding. Rough, rustic-looking cedar shakes are the more common choice for roofing. Shingles and shakes were once typically installed onto "skip" sheathing made of spaced boards, which allowed for air circulation and prevented moisture buildup, prolonging the life of the roof. That method is still commonly used (see below right), but many builders install them onto standard, solid sheathing.

A shake's or shingle's length determines its exposure (the part that is not covered by the shake that rests on top of it). An 18-inch-long shake should have a 7½-inch exposure; a 24-inch shake has a 10-inch exposure. Shingles have shorter exposures—for instance a 5½-inch exposure for an 18-inch-long shingle.

PRESTART CHECKLIST

☐ **TIME**
Working with a helper, 3 days to install flashings and roofing for a 700-square-foot roof with modest complications

☐ **TOOLS**
Tape measure, roofer's hatchet or nail gun, framing square, chalkline, circular saw, jigsaw, flat pry bar, caulk gun, utility knife, tin snips

☐ **SKILLS**
Basic carpentry

☐ **PREP**
Prepare the sheathing (either skip or solid) and apply WSU and flashings.

☐ **MATERIALS**
Shakes or shingles, ridgecaps, shake or shingle nails, WSU, roofing felt, interlay strips (for shakes only), flashings for valleys, chimneys, and walls (no drip edge is needed)

1 Prepare the sheathing and the underlayment. Consult your building department for the recommended sheathing and underlayment in your area. Apply WSU underlayment to the bottom 36 inches of the sheathing (which is solid even if the rest of the sheathing is skip-type). Allow the underlayment to overhang the sheathing by about ½ inch. Apply roofing felt or WSU and valley flashings as described on pages 40–43. No drip edge is used for the eaves or the rake ends.

SKIP AND SOLID SHEATHING

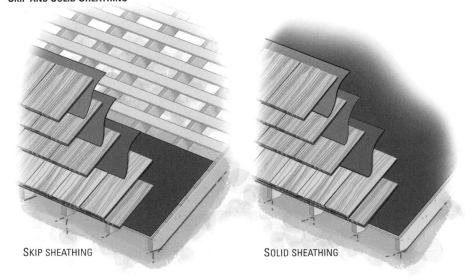

SKIP SHEATHING   SOLID SHEATHING

Skip sheathing, commonly used in wet climates, allows air to circulate below the shingles to remove trapped moisture. Skip sheathing is usually 1×4s with 4-inch spaces between them. Solid sheathing is more common in drier climes. With both types of sheathing, shakes are installed with 18-inch-wide strips of 15-pound felt, called interlays.

2 Install end shakes and a layout line. Install a shake, overhanging the sheathing by 1½ inches, at each end of the roof section. Tack a small nail into each and stretch a taut string line between them.

3 Install the starter course. The starter course is typically made of shakes that are shorter than regular shakes. Position the starters so they just barely miss touching the layout line. Maintain ½-inch gaps between the shakes.

4 The joints of the first course should be offset from the starter-course joints by at least 1½ inches. Install the ends flush with the bottom of the starter course. Drive two nails per shake, each about 1 inch from the side and 1½ inches above the exposure line.

The variety of shakes and shingles available varies regionally. Medium or heavy No. 1 hand-split shakes are the most common. You can buy pressure-treated shingles with a brownish tint or untreated ones. (The treatment will have to be reapplied every few years.)

5 Ideally a shingle should be cut with a power saw, but you can usually cut a shake by hand. To use a roofing hatchet, insert the blade at the top, pull down, and twist. The cut does not have to be perfectly straight. A block plane (inset) can clean up the split.

6 Snap two horizontal layout lines, one at the exposure line and a second that is twice the exposure distance.

7 Roll 18-inch-wide interlay strips over the tops of the shakes, following the upper layout line (Step 6). Pull the interlay strip taut so that there are no creases or bubbles. Fasten with staples driven near the top every foot or so.

8 Continue installing courses. Aim to drive the nails just flush with the wood surface; do not dimple the wood with the hatchet head or drive the nails below the surface with a power nailer. Avoid the temptation to install more than two nails per shake— no matter how wide it is.

STANLEY PRO TIP: **Make a roofer's seat**

This handy seat can be used for wood shakes only; it will damage all other types of roofing. Build the sides and top out of ½-inch or ¾-inch plywood. Use a level to determine the slope at which to cut the side pieces and attach the top piece. On the bottom install two 1×6 crosspieces. Drive 1-inch roofing nails through the 1×6s; they will poke through just enough to grab the shakes and make a stable seat (see page 59).

ALIGNING SHAKES

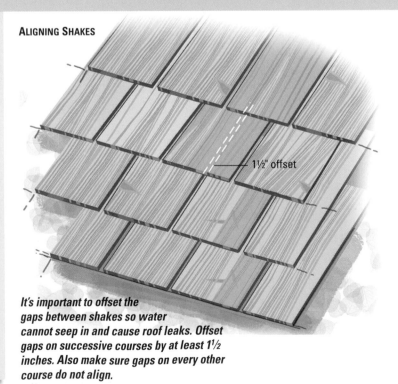

1½" offset

It's important to offset the gaps between shakes so water cannot seep in and cause roof leaks. Offset gaps on successive courses by at least 1½ inches. Also make sure gaps on every other course do not align.

9 The exposure guide on the hatchet is not long enough for shakes. To ease marking for chalklines, make a simple guide using a piece of scrap wood notched with the recommended exposure (see the introductory text on page 56).

10 You can install succeeding courses using the layout line, but a nailing guide is quick to install and ensures straight lines. Tack a long, straight 1×4 or other board against the exposure line and set the next course of shakes against it.

11 With practice you will learn how to place shakes on the roof so they will be in easy reach; one approach is shown above. With a gentler slope bundles can be simply laid on the roof.

STANLEY PRO TIP: **Installing multiple courses**

Installing one whole course at a time is a sure way to success; but the going can be slow and you'll spend lots of time moving around on your knees. Once you have the hang of the basic process, you may choose to install multiple courses at once. Roll out three or more rolls of interlay and slip the shakes under them as you work.

12 To mark for cutting shakes at a valley, hold a 1×4 against the valley flashing center ridge. (There is no need to widen the gap in the shakes as you proceed down the roof.) You may have to trim the shake before marking.

13 Install shakes at a valley using a 1×4 as a spacer. When installing shakes near valley flashing, do not drive nails closer to the center ridge than 12 inches. You will need to drive some nails higher than usual.

14 As you near the ridge, measure at several places to see that the courses remain parallel to the ridge. If the rows are getting off-kilter, snap lines to take out the difference over several courses so that it will not be noticeable.

WHAT IF...
You meet a vent pipe?

1 When you come to a pipe or other obstruction, plan ahead so you don't have narrow pieces on either side. Cut the lower piece to fit around the pipe with a ¾-inch gap to allow for expansion.

2 Prepare the flashing to fit over the pipe, apply roofing cement to its underside, and install the flashing over the lower row (see page 48).

3 Roof over the sides and top of the flashing. Cut the shakes to fit, again maintaining a ¾-inch gap. With smaller flashing, you may be able to use one very wide shake.

15 Roof up to one side of the ridge. Place the shakes so they run past the peak. Snap a chalkline about 1 inch below the peak and cut the shakes with a circular saw. Set the saw's blade to just barely cut through the shakes so you don't damage the underlayment or sheathing. Then attach shakes on the opposite side as shown, again letting them run past the peak.

16 Strike a chalkline to guide you in cutting the shingles. Make sure that all the shingles rest flat on the roof and that none protrude past the peak.

17 Buy ridgecap pieces, which are uniform in width and have beveled edges. Hold two pieces of ridgecap in place at each end and mark their edges. Snap layout lines on each side between the marks.

18 Align pairs of caps with the layout lines and attach them by driving extra-long nails. The exposure should be the same as for the rest of the roof—use your notched exposure guide. Alternate the overlaps of the ridgecaps as shown.

VERTICAL METAL ROOFING

Metal roofing installs quickly and lasts a long time, making it worth its somewhat higher cost. Metal roofing comes in shingles and in horizontal strips that look like shingles, but the most popular type involves vertical roofing panels like the ones shown in these steps.

Most metal roofing products get very hot when the sun shines but cool off quickly in the shade. Overheating is usually not a problem, but you can buy metal roofing designed to stay relatively cool. Contrary to some homeowners' concerns, a metal roof installed onto roof sheathing and felt is not particularly noisy.

Consult with your dealer when purchasing metal roofing. Some types require a minimum pitch. Vertical roofing can be difficult—even dangerous—to install if the pitch is too steep. In most cases nearly everything that goes on the roof—panels, various flashings, ridgecap, and sealant—will be made and cut to size by the same manufacturer.

1 Metal roofing is not heavy so you can apply it over shingles. However many installers prefer to tear off the old roofing so they can thoroughly inspect the sheathing first. Apply 30-pound felt and WSU (pages 40–41). Be sure to use special high-temperature WSU; standard WSU can melt under a metal roof. Also install eave flashing in advance.

2 Install the valley flashing as shown on pages 42–43 or according to manufacturer's instructions. In most cases the panels attach to the valley flashing using sealant.

PRESTART CHECKLIST

☐ **TIME**
Once the sheathing and underlayment is prepared, about a day for two people to install a 700-square-foot roof.

☐ **TOOLS**
Tape measure, drill with screwdriver bit, hammer, framing square, two pairs of tin snips or a nibbler tool, bending pliers, flat pry bar, caulking gun

☐ **SKILLS**
Basic carpentry skills, careful measuring

☐ **PREP**
Tear off roofing if needed (see pages 36–37) and carefully measure the roof.

☐ **MATERIALS**
Metal roofing panels, flashings, ridgecap, sealant or caulk, 30-pound roofing felt and staples, metal and wood screws as specified by the manufacturer

STANLEY PRO TIP: **Cutting metal roofing**

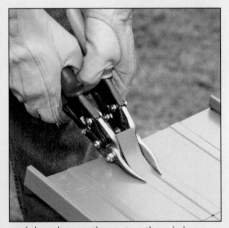

Most panels will be cut to length by the manufacturer, but you will probably need to cut some panels to width at rake ends, where they meet a valley, and to fit around obstructions. You could cut them using a circular saw or jigsaw equipped with a metal-cutting blade, but that would expose the cut edge and invite rust; tin snips actually seal the edges as they cut so there is less chance of rust.

If you have curved or intricate cuts to make, consider renting a metal-cutting nibbler, as shown (above left). To make a long, straight cut, use two snips, one left-handed and one right-handed, as shown (above). Make short cuts with a single pair of tin snips.

3 While it is possible to order panels in advance, you'll get the most accurate measurements if you wait until the flashing is installed. If you have gutters the roofing should overhang the eave by no more than 1½ inches; if there is no gutter it can overhang by 3 inches or so. If the roof measurements vary, you can likely make up the difference at the ridge.

4 The panels are durable once installed, but they can bend during handling. Store them laid flat, either weighted or wrapped, so they cannot blow away. Work with a helper when lifting them onto the roof.

5 Ensure that the first panel overhangs the eave by the correct distance. Drive screws through the panel's flange and into the underlayment. Drive into the middle of the nailing hole to allow the panel to move when it expands and contracts.

6 Some manufacturers recommend that you snap chalklines for the layout, but in most cases you need to align only the first piece correctly and the others will follow. It is very important to get the first piece perpendicular to the eave and the ridge. Place the panel in position and check for square using the "3-4-5" method: Mark a point on the panel 3 feet up from the eave and a point on the eave that is 4 feet from the panel. If the distance between the two marks is exactly 5 feet, then the panel is square; if not adjust and remeasure. For greater accuracy use multiples of 3, 4, and 5 (such as 6, 8, 10—or even 30, 40, 50).

STANLEY PRO TIP

Insulating and sealing a metal roof

For a standard roof with an attic below, there is no need to install insulation. However if the room below has a ceiling that follows the roofline, inquire about the possibility of installing insulation over the roof before adding the roofing.

A metal roof typically has ribs that create small openings along the eave and other places—inviting places for wasps and other insects to live. You may choose to seal these openings with a bead of either the manufacturer's sealant or butyl caulk.

7 Have a helper align the next panel at the eave, as you press with your thumb or palm to snap its rib over the rib of the first piece. Drive screws as for the first piece. Repeat until you reach the last piece, which will probably need to be rip-cut to fit.

8 Where the panels meet a valley, hold them in place and use a straightedge to mark for cutting, then cut with tin snips. Apply two beads of sealant (either using a caulk tube or by applying strips provided by the manufacturer) and set the panels in the sealant. Do not drive screws through the valley flashing.

9 Where a pipe or other obstruction pokes through, cut the panel so that a ½-inch gap is left between it and the obstruction. Prepare the flashing—in this case a rubber boot with a flange that must be cut off to fit the pipe size.

WHAT IF...
A pipe is in the middle of a ridge or seam?

Where a pipe pokes through at a seam or rib, cut the rubber boot as directed so that it can rest at different levels on either side. Wrap the rubber with the clamps provided, apply sealant, and drive self-sealing screws.

13 Fit the rake flashing tightly against the bottom of the panel at the rake. Apply sealant as recommended and drive screws to fasten the flashing to the rake fascia.

14 At the ends you will need to snip and fold sidewall and endwall flashing to fit, similar to the rake flashing (Steps 11 and 12). Pry out the house's siding (you may have to temporarily remove it) and tuck the flashing up under the siding.

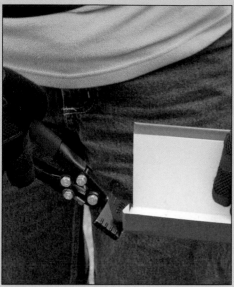

10 Slide the boot down over the pipe to make sure it fits. Apply sealant or butyl caulk to the roof, set the flashing in the sealant, and drive self-sealing screws to attach it. Check around the flashing base and apply additional sealant as needed for a complete seal.

11 At various points you'll need to snip and fold flashings so they seal tightly over the panels. Use tin snips to cut a rake flashing piece as shown so that you will have tabs that can protect the exposed ends of the panel.

12 Use broad pliers (known as hand seamers) to carefully bend the tabs to create a tight seam. You will need to make a final small cut at the bottom.

15 Various ridgecaps will likely be available to suit different situations. Choose the one that calls for the least amount of cutting; with some types you need to cut many little V notches to fit over the panels on either side. Fold the edges on both ends, similar to Steps 11 and 12, and drive self-sealing screws as instructed.

STANLEY PRO TIP

Other installation methods

Some manufacturers may recommend installation methods that vary from the directions shown on these pages. For instance you may need to install a starter strip along the eave for some roofing.

Where high winds are a problem, it is sometimes recommended to drive additional screws along the eave in the middle of the panels. These screws should be self-sealing or should be covered with sealant.

In some cases you may need to create a new rib for the rake flashing to fit over at the ending rake. Consult with your dealer or hire a sheet-metal shop to make this rib for you.

FAUX TILES

A variety of faux tiles can be ordered through a home center, building supply store, or online source. You will likely need to order the materials and wait a few weeks for delivery. Many faux tiles are made to imitate slate or cedar shakes; others have solid colors for a more contemporary look. Many of these products are made of recycled tires. They are expensive but will last a long time; some have a lifetime warranty.

Bring a drawing of your roof to the dealer and buy all the parts, including field tiles, flashings, and ridge tiles. These tiles are not heavy so standard sheathing is usually strong enough. You can reroof with faux tiles (pages 32–35), but many roofers prefer to tear off first so they can give the sheathing a good inspection and make needed repairs. Prepare the roof and layout for the tiles as you would for composition shingles (pages 40–43).

PRESTART CHECKLIST

☐ **TIME**
Once the sheathing and underlayment are prepared, about a day to tile a 700-square-foot roof, working with a helper

☐ **TOOLS**
Tape measure, hammer or pneumatic nailer, framing square, utility knife, chalkline, flat pry bar, caulking gun

☐ **SKILLS**
Careful measuring, cutting, fastening

☐ **PREP**
Tear off roofing if needed (see pages 36–37) and carefully measure the roof. Buy all the components recommended by the tile dealer.

☐ **MATERIALS**
Felt and WSU, flashings, field tiles, ridge tiles, recommended nails (perhaps stainless-steel), roofing cement

1 Cover the roof with WSU at the eaves and 30-pound felt elsewhere (see pages 40–41). Install drip-edge flashing at the eaves and valley flashing if needed (pages 42–43). Use flashings recommended by the tile dealer. Snap a chalkline to help maintain a straight course. Tiles should overhang the drip edge by ¼ inch or so.

2 Install a starter row of tiles. These can be installed in a standard way or upside down, as recommended by the manufacturer. Drive nails as indicated on the tiles.

PATTERN OPTIONS FOR FAKE SLATE

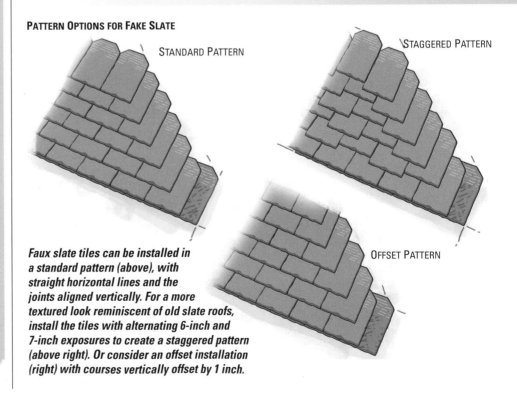

STANDARD PATTERN

STAGGERED PATTERN

OFFSET PATTERN

Faux slate tiles can be installed in a standard pattern (above), with straight horizontal lines and the joints aligned vertically. For a more textured look reminiscent of old slate roofs, install the tiles with alternating 6-inch and 7-inch exposures to create a staggered pattern (above right). Or consider an offset installation (right) with courses vertically offset by 1 inch.

3 Attach the first-course tiles directly on top of the starter tiles, offset so their joints are at least 3 inches away from the starter-course joints. Drive the nails flush, but not so deep that they cause the bottom edges to lift up. (If using a power nailer, you may need to adjust it to achieve the right amount of force.)

4 Lay out the tiles using either the pyramid or racked method (see pages 44–45). Snap at least one vertical layout line, perpendicular to the roof, and horizontal lines for every three or four courses.

5 Where there is no horizontal chalkline, use the exposure lines imprinted on the tiles as a guide for alignment, then drive two nails for each tile. Use alternating 6-inch and 7-inch exposures for a staggered installation. For an offset installation place every other course 1 inch to the left or right of the vertical line.

6 To cut a tile hold a straightedge on your cutline and cut it repeatedly with a utility knife. Mark tiles at the valley as shown on page 60.

7 If the tiles come in different colors or even with subtly different textures, you may need to shuffle them in order to achieve a pleasingly random effect.

8 Preformed ridge tiles make it easy to cover the ridge. Install them with a 6-inch exposure. Nearly all the nailheads will be covered; seal any exposed heads with dabs of roofing cement.

TILE ROOFS

Although concrete tiles are costly and hard work to install, they are often warranted for 50 years. Some tile roofs have lasted 100 years.

Concrete tiles come in a variety of weights. Check with your dealer and local building department to make sure your roof is strong enough to support the weight of the tiles.

Unlike a composition shingle roof, a tile roof does not actually seal out all the water. Some moisture flows down through channels in the tile, and some moisture even seeps down to the underlayment where it runs under the tiles and out at the eaves. This means that flashings must be installed correctly. If you are unsure about a flashing arrangement, consult a professional.

The tiles you choose may call for different parts and techniques. Be sure that your dealer supplies you with all the parts you need—tiles, ridgecaps, rake caps, and various types of flashings.

PRESTART CHECKLIST

☐ **TIME**
   Two or three days, working with a helper, to install underlayment and tiles for a 700-square-foot roof

☐ **TOOLS**
   Tape measure, hammer, roofing hatchet, tile cutter or circular saw with masonry blade, chalkline, caulking gun, drill, trowel

☐ **SKILLS**
   Basic roofing skills, plus an understanding of flashing techniques for tiles

☐ **PREP**
   Measure and make a drawing of the roof and have a dealer supply you with advice and all the parts you need.

☐ **MATERIALS**
   Heavy roofing felt, WSU, field tiles, hip caps, ridgecaps, rake caps, various types of flashings, 2×4 for the ridge, 1×2 battens, nails for battens and tiles, metal eave riser, mastic approved by the tile manufacturer, vented tile tape

1 Install WSU and extra-heavy roofing felt (see pages 40–41). Most codes call for 30-pound ASTM felt, which is heavier than standard 30-pound felt. Run the felt past the rake and staple it to the fascia.

2 Cut and attach the valley flashing that's recommended by your tilemaker; ribbed W-valley flashing is often the best choice because it has ample channels to keep water from seeping under the tiles. In some tile arrangements you will also need to install eave flashings (see page 70). Allow 2 inches for tile overhang at the eave.

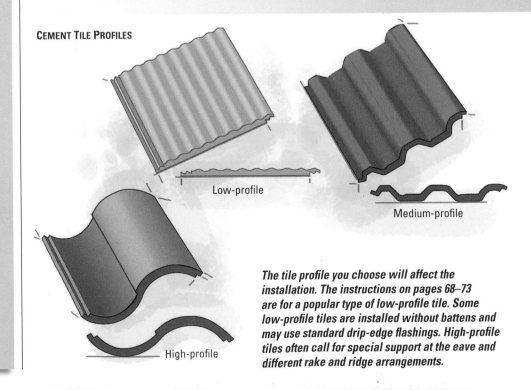

CEMENT TILE PROFILES

Low-profile

Medium-profile

High-profile

The tile profile you choose will affect the installation. The instructions on pages 68–73 are for a popular type of low-profile tile. Some low-profile tiles are installed without battens and may use standard drip-edge flashings. High-profile tiles often call for special support at the eave and different rake and ridge arrangements.

3 At a sidewall you cannot install flashing on top of the tiles (as you would for composition shingles). Instead use pan flashing, also called J-metal. Water will seep between the wall and the tile, and the flashing will carry it down the roof, much like valley flashing.

4 Chimney flashing for a tile roof is complicated, so either get detailed instructions from your dealer or hire a pro. The backer piece and side pieces are typically installed before the battens.

5 The top and bottom tiles must be full-size, so you must adjust the tile exposure so the courses come out even. Position a tile at the eave, overhanging by 2 inches, and one at the top 1½ inches from the peak. Measure from tile to tile and move the top tile sideways until you come out with an even number of exposures. Mark the roof for each batten.

FLEXIBLE CHIMNEY FLASHING

Chimneys are typically flashed with pan metal at the top and the sides to channel water down and keep it from seeping onto the roof. Near the bottom the flashing moves up onto the tiles. For those spots flexible lead flashing is sometimes used because it can be molded to the shape of the tiles.

HEAD WALL FLASHING

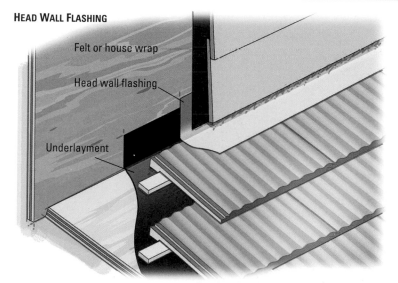

Felt or house wrap

Head wall flashing

Underlayment

At a head wall flashing slips behind the siding and rests on top of the tiles. You may be able to buy head flashings that fit the contours of your tiles.

6 Working with a helper, chalk layout lines indicating the top of each batten course. Also chalk two or more vertical layout lines on the right side of the roof, where you will start laying tiles, to help you maintain straight joint lines (see page 45).

7 Most commonly 4-foot-long 1×2 battens made of cedar or pressure-treated wood are installed with 1½-inch gaps between them to allow water to run down the roof. If you live in an area that gets strong rains, consider installing counterbattens (see illustration below left).

WHAT IF...
You live in a rainy area?

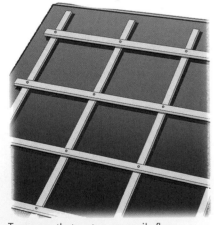

To ensure that water can easily flow beneath the tiles, in some areas it is common to first install vertical counterbattens with horizontal battens attached on top. Codes typically require that the counterbattens be spaced no more than 2 feet apart; 1×2 battens are not strong enough to span a longer distance.

OTHER EAVE ARRANGEMENTS

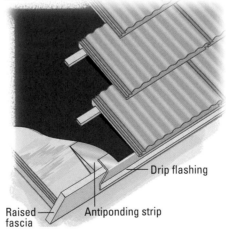

Drip flashing

Raised fascia — Antiponding strip

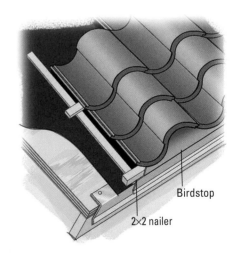

Birdstop

2×2 nailer

Eaves can be finished in a variety of ways depending on the shape of the tiles. Here are two of the most common methods. For the raised fascia method (above), remove the fascia and reinstall it so that it protrudes 1½ inches above the eave. Install drip edge as recommended. You also may need to install a metal antiponding strip before installing the underlayment, battens, and tiles.

If your tiles have a high profile, install a 2×2 nailer near the eave. After laying the first course of tiles, slip in special metal birdstop molding, made to fit the tile's profile. Cover the lower portion of the birdstop with metal flashing.

8 Depending on the type of tile, you may need to install two 2×2s (less likely to warp than a 2×4) at the ridge. The 2×2s may come flush to the rake or may need to overhang by a certain amount. Drill angled pilot holes before driving nails or screws. Or use metal angle brackets and screws for a stronger connection (see page 72).

9 The initial placement of tiles is actually an important part of the job. Follow the manufacturer's instructions (there may be an illustration showing where to put them) for placing stacks of tiles so you can easily reach them while working.

10 The bottom edge of the first course typically should be raised 1½ inches. To accomplish this you may be able to buy a metal eave riser shaped to fit the tile's profile. Cut the riser with a hacksaw or tin snips, position it along with the first tile, and drive nails or screws to attach the riser. Drive nails to attach the first tile.

11 Most tiles fit together by setting a lip on the right side into a groove on the left side of the previous tile. Restrike chalklines as you go around obstructions. Drive nails through the holes and into battens. Take care not to overdrive, which can cause the bottom of the tile to lift up.

12 Follow the manufacturer's directions for cutting tile. If the cut does not have to be precise, you can often chop off a piece using a roofing hatchet. Otherwise use a tile cutter (shown) or circular saw equipped with a masonry-cutting blade. Be sure to protect your eyes, ears, and hands.

13 In a common arrangement, a vent pipe is first flashed with a lead jack that is glued and nailed to the underlayment; then a collar flashing is installed so its top rests on the flashing and its bottom rests on the lower tiles. You may be able to buy vent-pipe collar flashing that fits the profile of your tiles.

14 Lift up the bottom of the collar, apply mastic or roofing cement, and press the collar down so it embeds completely. Once the collar is installed, apply roofing cement for the surrounding tiles.

15 Cut the surrounding tiles so that they fit fairly snugly but not so they abut the pipe itself. Set the bottoms of these tiles in mastic or roofing cement. Avoid piercing the flashing with fasteners.

OTHER RIDGE ARRANGEMENTS

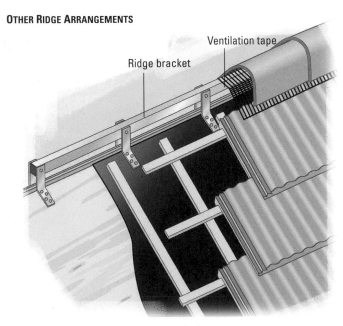

If the roof has a ridge vent, a 2×2 is used instead of a 2×4 and is raised using brackets to allow for an air space. Ventilation tape is applied over the brackets and onto the field tiles, and then the ridgecaps are attached.

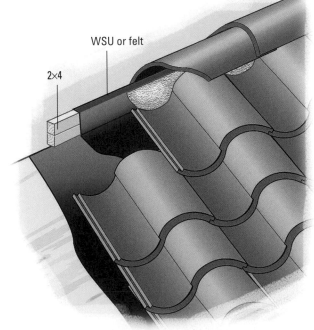

With some high-profile tiles (above), it is common to first wrap the 2×4 with WSU or felt, install the caps, then seal all the joints with mortar.

16 Once you have tiled up to the ridge on each side, follow the manufacturer's directions for sealing the ridgecaps. In a typical arrangement you'll first spread approved mastic on the 2×4 and the top edges of the tiles, then embed special vented tile tape along the ridge.

17 Apply the ridgecaps over the tile tape. Embed the tiles in a bead of silicone caulk, mastic, or roofing cement, and drive nails to attach the tiles. You may need a hip starter (next step) or a similar piece at the beginning and/or end of the rake. Set the last piece in mastic.

18 Hips may be finished using ridgecaps or similar pieces. You typically need to start with a hip starter, which has a finished (bullnose) edge. Set the caps in mastic or cement, driving nails wherever possible.

19 At the rake end you may use ridgecaps or special rake caps (shown). These are often nailed to the fascia and set in mastic or cement. Where the rake meets the ridge, finish with a ridgecap.

MODIFIED-BITUMEN ROOFING

Flat roofs were once exclusively the province of professionals, but new materials enable do-it-yourselfers to install flat roofs. If your flat roof is covered with gravel, you will likely need to hire a professional to reroof it. If the surface is smooth you may be able to reroof using sheets of modified bitumen (pages 74–79) or EPDM (rubber) roofing (below right).

Consult with your inspector to see whether you need to tear off the old roofing or if you can reroof over the existing roofing. Use flashings approved by your building department. Modified-bitumen roofing may have a granular surface as shown here or it may be smooth. If you install the smooth product, cover it with aluminum coating as shown on page 90.

These steps show a "torch-down" method, which looks a bit scary but actually is not difficult. Renting a large propane torch is inexpensive. You can also set the sheets in adhesive; this sounds easier but is actually messier and more time-consuming.

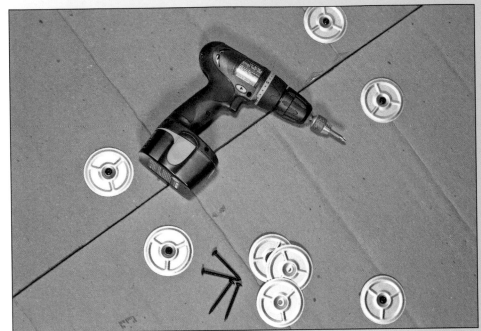

1 Remove all obstructions and sweep the roof clean of debris. You may need to remove old flashings.

If your roof is not already insulated, it is usually worth the time and expense to lay sheets of rigid insulation made for a flat roof. Cut them to fit fairly tightly and make sure that you will support the flashing pieces at the ends. Attach the insulation with fasteners as recommended by the manufacturer—in this case hold-down plates and specially-coated screws long enough to penetrate the decking.

PRESTART CHECKLIST

☐ **TIME**
One or two days, working with a helper, to lay insulation and modified-bitumen roofing for a 500-square-foot roof

☐ **TOOLS**
Tape measure, hammer, chalkline, large propane torch, utility knife with hook blade, spark igniter

☐ **SKILLS**
Measuring, cutting, using a torch

☐ **PREP**
Measure and make a drawing of the roof and consult with a dealer.

☐ **MATERIALS**
Roof insulation, heavy roofing felt, modified-bitumen roofing, drip-edge and other flashings, spray primer, cap nails, roofing nails, roofing cement

WHAT IF...
You install an EPDM (rubber) roof?

Single-ply rubber (or EPDM) roofing is fairly quick to install and can last a long time. It is typically installed using an adhesive that acts like contact cement. Cut each piece to fit, then reroll it halfway, apply the adhesive, and roll it back onto the roof carefully— it is difficult to adjust its position once it is stuck down.

2 Apply extra-heavy (typically 43-pound) roofing felt over the sheathing, old roof, or the insulation. See pages 40–41. Drive cap nails 6 to 8 inches apart in rows along the top and bottom of the sheets, as well as in a row in the middle.

3 Attach drip-edge flashings as needed (see pages 42–43). You will install rake-end flashings later (Step 21). Use wide flashings approved for use with a flat roof and attach them with roofing nails every 8 to 12 inches.

4 To ensure that the roofing will stick firmly to the flashing, spray the flange of the flashing with a special primer.

5 Roll out a sheet of roofing. Allow it to overhang the rake or side of the roof by a couple of inches; you will cut it precisely to length later (Step 20). Take care to avoid bubbles or creases.

6 Cut the roofing roughly to length, again allowing it to overhang by a couple of inches.

7 Adjust the position of the sheet so that it overhangs the drip-edge flashing by ½ inch or so all along its length. Check that the roofing lies perfectly flat.

8 Taking care not to move the roofing out of position as you work, reroll the roofing halfway. Keep the roll fairly tight so that it will roll back neatly (Step 10).

9 Turn on the gas and light the torch, using a spark igniter. Wear heavy gloves and long sleeves to protect yourself from the heat. Adjust the torch so it produces a concentrated flame that is mostly blue.

STANLEY PRO TIP: **Working with a propane torch**

Place the propane tank in a central location so that you can work across the roof without having to move the tank during the installation of a sheet.

The tank may ice up (propane acts like a refrigerant), which will cause the flame to

diminish. If this happens lift the tank and lightly heat it with the torch (left).

If you set the nozzle onto the felt while it is still hot, it may melt the felt or set it on fire. Protect the roof with a rag, set it on a leather work glove (center), or overhang the nozzle

beyond the roof (right).

At all times pay attention to the nozzle when it is flaming or hot. It is possible to start a fire on the roof if you leave a hot or flaming nozzle unattended.

10 Run the tip of the flame along the intersection of the roofing roll and the sheathing; the idea is to lightly melt both the roofing and the felt. Once you see heat bubbles along the roll's width, use your foot to gently roll the roofing forward.

11 Take your time rolling and heating so that the roofing is heat-adhered at all points. Take special care to produce tight seals at the ends. Often you can use the spark igniter as a tool to gently lift up an end while you apply heat.

12 Along the flashing and at the rake end, press down with your foot to ensure a tight seal.

13 Align the next sheets so they cover the unfinished top edges. Because the sheets are wide, you usually do not need to worry about precise alignment of each sheet in relation to the ridge.

14 Torch and roll succeeding sheets the way you did the first sheet. Take special care to fully heat the seam between the sheets.

15 Press with your feet, then a gloved hand, to tighten the seal at the seam between the sheets. A small amount of melted black sealant should ooze out all along the joint.

16 At a vertical seam (or butt joint), fully seal the first piece onto the underlayment. Cut the next piece so it overlaps by 4 to 6 inches. Align the second sheet and torch and roll it toward the first.

17 Complete a vertical seam by pressing with gloved hands, making sure that a small amount of melted black sealant oozes out all along the joint.

18 If you have a ridge, first install sheets on each side. Position a sheet along a ridge and cut it lengthwise so it will just overlap the seam seal.

19 Torch one side of the ridge, then the other. Take special care to make tight, fully adhered seams.

20 Cut rake ends flush with the outside edge of the sheathing. You can use a chalkline for this, but it is usually not necessary because the rake will be covered with flashing (next step).

21 Install drip-edge flashing along the rakes and spray with primer.

22 Cut a number of strips, about 8 inches wide, to cover the rake flashing. Use a chalkline and tape measure to make precise cuts only if the roof will be highly visible.

23 Starting at the bottom, position the strips so they overhang the flashing by ½ inch or so. Torch the pieces onto the flashing and the roofing.

24 Press the strips firmly into place. When you reach the ridge, cut and install a strip that is the same length as the width of the ridge sheet.

STANLEY PRO TIP: **Tying into an adjoining roof**

If a flat roof meets a sloped roof, be sure to configure the flashings and roofing pieces so water has no opportunity to infiltrate as it flows downward. In some cases this means that flashings will direct water onto the sloped roof.

If the old roof worked well, copy its flashing and roofing arrangement. Visualize how water will flow and avoid places where water can puddle or flow under an overlapping roofing piece.

If you have a short parapet wall, you can

usually roll the roofing sheets up onto it. The sheets cannot make a tight turn, so there should be flashing or built-up roofing in the corners so the roofing can make a gentle, sweeping turn upward. Seal the top of the roofing completely.

ROLL ROOFING

For a utilitarian solution when appearance isn't as important, consider roll roofing, which is made of materials similar to composition shingles but generally not as durable. Be sure to check the warranty, which may be for only one year. If you install roll roofing using the double-coverage method (see the tip on page 81), it will last longer.

Roll roofing is often installed over bare wood sheathing or sheathing that has been painted with a primer. Applying roofing felt first will better protect the sheathing against condensation, as well as against leaking.

If the roof is sloped, you can use the exposed-nail method shown on pages 80 and 81. For a slightly sloped roof, use the concealed-nail method shown in the box, below right. For a flat or nearly flat roof, use double coverage, although a torch-down modified bitumen or EPDM roof (see pages 74–79) is a better solution.

PRESTART CHECKLIST

☐ **TIME**
Working with a helper, half a day to install flashings and roll roofing for a 700-square-foot roof with modest complications

☐ **TOOLS**
Hammer or power nailer, tape measure, flat pry bar, carpenter's square, tin snips, utility knife, chalkline, broom

☐ **SKILLS**
This is the least difficult of roofing materials to install: Only basic carpentry skills are needed.

☐ **PREP**
Prepare the roof by tearing off the old shingles (pages 36–37), or by preparing for a reroof (page 32).

☐ **MATERIALS**
Flashing, nails for flashing, roofing felt or primer, perhaps WSU for the eaves, roll roofing, nails long enough to poke through the sheathing, roofing cement

1 Install drip-edge flashings, roofing felt, and perhaps WSU (see pages 40–41). You can install metal valley flashing, but it is common to simply apply an 18-inch-wide strip of roll roofing instead. Set it in a bed of roofing cement, smooth out any creases, and drive nails near the edges.

2 Position the first course so it overhangs the drip edges by about ¼ inch and roll it out a distance of 8 feet or so. Drive nails every 3 inches along the rake at one end, pull it taut, and drive nails along the eave edge. The nails should be about 1 inch from the edges. For extra protection add a 3-foot-wide strip on top of the 18-incher.

WHAT IF...
You have a slightly sloped roof?

1 Cut strips of roofing 9 inches wide, position them flush with the drip edges along the eave and rake, and attach them by driving two rows of nails that are about 3 inches apart. Use a trowel to spread roofing cement over half or more of the strips.

2 Set the first course in the cement so it overhangs by about ¼ inch. Position and roll out the roofing carefully because it is not easy to reposition, then press it into the cement. Nail only its top edge (the part that is bare of mineral coating). Coat the top edge with a 4- to 6-inch-wide layer of roofing cement and apply the next courses in the same way.

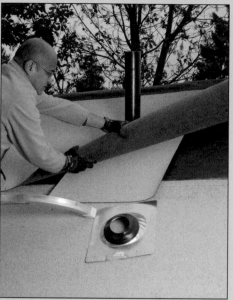

3 The next sheet overlaps the first by 4 inches or with some types of roll roofing, enough to cover the area that is bare of mineral surfacing. Snap a chalkline indicating the top of the next sheet, roll it out along the line, and drive nails as for the first sheet.

4 Plan so that no two butt joints are closer than 2 feet from each other. Spread a 6-inch-wide layer of roofing cement on the edge of the first sheet and embed the next sheet in the cement.

5 To seal a plumbing vent, spread roofing cement around the pipe. Cut a hole in a piece of roofing about 2 feet wide and slip it over the pipe. The piece should overlap the lower course by at least 4 inches. Cut a hole in the roll roofing and slip it over as well. Embed both roofing pieces in cement. For added protection add a boot flashing.

6 Work from one side roof past the center of a valley by 2 feet. Then, working from the other side, overlap the valley, strike a chalkline, and trim the piece at the center of the valley. Keep nails at least 12 inches from the center of the valley; use a 4-inch-wide bed of roofing cement to attach everything that is closer than 12 inches.

7 In most cases you can simply overlap the sheets at the ridge using roofing cement and nails for the final piece. However if the final piece does not come down at least 8 inches past the peak, cover the peak with a 16-inch-wide strip that is embedded in cement.

WHAT IF...
You want double coverage?

For the greatest protection apply two layers of roll roofing. In some parts of the country you can buy selvage roofing, which has only half its width covered with minerals; the bare portion gets covered by the coated portion of the upper sheet. However you can double cover a roof using standard roll roofing.

Start by nailing on a half-wide sheet. Apply 6-inch-wide strips of roofing cement to the starter sheet and embed the next (full-width) sheet in the cement. Nail its top edges only. Repeat for the other sheets.

ROOF REPAIRS

A leaking roof can cause serious and costly damage to your house. Infiltrating water can destroy drywall or plaster, cause mold, and even rot framing. You should repair a roof as soon as possible after the damage occurs.

Dealing with a damaged roof is sometimes a simple matter of applying roofing cement to an obvious hole; at other times you will need to spend time diagnosing the problem and calculating the benefits of repairs versus installing a new roof. This chapter will guide you through repairs for all types of roofs.

Roofing diagnostics and triage

If a roof starts to leak, determine whether it is worthwhile to make permanent repairs or whether you need to apply new roofing. Here are your choices:

■ If the roof is basically sound with only one or two weak spots, the damage may have come from a falling branch or a particularly severe windstorm. In that case make permanent repairs.

■ If the roof shows signs of general wear, making repairs will solve the problem only temporarily; other leaks will soon appear. Start planning a reroof.

■ If you can reroof soon but need a few weeks to plan and prepare, cover leaks with plywood or plastic sheets until you can start.

■ If you need to wait a year or so, make permanent repairs now, such as replacing shingles. Inspect the attic after every rainfall and make further repairs or take steps to protect your interior spaces from water damage.

The importance of flashing

Often the culprit is not the roofing itself but the flashing that protects the joints between roofing and chimneys or walls. Valleys, which may or may not have flashing, are often a trouble spot.

If you have a longstanding problem, repairs can be tricky; it's not unusual for a roofer to make three or four attempts before finally fixing a chronic leak. In other cases the solution is obvious: A piece of flashing may be rusted through, may be missing, or may have come loose. Often you can simply apply roofing cement or a new piece of metal flashing to solve the problem.

This chapter will help you identify flashing problems, make some of the most common repairs, and determine when it is time to call in a pro.

Attic ventilation

A roof must breathe or moisture from the air will be trapped in the attic, ruining insulation and leading to mold and rot. This chapter will help you understand the principles of attic ventilation and show you how to install the most common venting products.

Infiltrating water can destroy drywall or plaster, cause mold, and even rot framing.

CHAPTER PREVIEW

Identifying problems
page 84

Spot and emergency repairs
page 86

Replacing shingles and shakes
page 88

Repairs to a flat roof
page 90

Asphalt roofing can lose its granule coating with age and, especially on the sunny side of the roof, become cracked and brittle. Careful replacement of damaged shingles will often let you eke out a few extra years of service before you have to reroof.

Flashing repairs
page 92

Chimney repairs
page 94

Venting an attic
page 96

Installing attic vents
page 98

IDENTIFYING PROBLEMS

A roof should be inspected yearly for signs of damage so that you can seal weak spots before water starts leaking into your living spaces. Here is how to make a quick and effective roof inspection:

Look for any tree branches that reach within 5 feet or so of the roof; they could scrape the roofing during a severe storm. Cut the branches back.

Watch for gutters that are stopped with leaves or other debris. These may become overfull, causing water to seep under the shingles during a rain. Worse, in the winter, freezing water can do serious damage to the roofing. See pages 178–185 for gutter repairs and installations.

■ In cold climates look for ice dams—a common problem that can result in serious damage. Icicles, however pretty, can be a symptom of this condition. (See the illustration at right.)

If roofing comes loose during heavy winds, it may not have been installed correctly. Consult a professional roofer.

Check the overall condition of the roofing, flashing, and attic ceiling. The photos on these pages will help you identify some of the more common types of problems.

Do not walk on a roof unless you are certain of your safety; see pages 22–25. Avoid walking on a composition shingle roof when it is very hot; doing so could scrape away mineral coatings, weakening the shingles. Also stay off when it is very cold to avoid cracking the shingles. Stay off tile and slate roofs, especially if they are old, because they can crack.

If shingles have lost much of their mineral coating (you may find particles falling on the yard below) or if several are cracked, it is probably time to reroof.

Cupping occurs when the adhesive holding the shingle tabs down has lost its ability to hold. Cupped shingles can be easily damaged in a windstorm and water can infiltrate beneath, possibly damaging the sheathing and even the house framing.

HOW ICE DAMS FORM

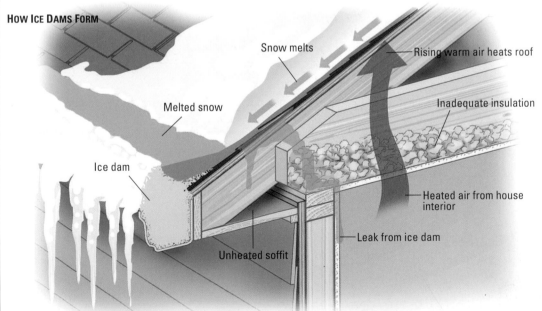

Snow melts

Rising warm air heats roof

Melted snow

Inadequate insulation

Ice dam

Heated air from house interior

Leak from ice dam

Unheated soffit

If you see ice collecting along your eaves, perhaps accompanied by long icicles, you likely have an ice dam. Ice dams form when insufficient insulation in the attic allows heat to rise. As that warms the attic space, snow on the roof can melt and trickle down to the eave. Because the eave is unheated, it freezes there, creating a dam. As melting water pools it

tends to seep under shingles where it can damage the roofing, the sheathing, and the attic framing. The solution is to keep the attic roof cold in the winter by adding insulation to the attic floor, a solution that will also help keep your heating costs down. In addition you may need to provide better ventilation for the attic; see pages 96–101.

Wood shakes or shingles may split due to freeze-thaw cycles or intense heat. Applying a sealer can forestall this. However once the shakes are damaged severely, they need to be replaced (see pages 88–89). Black mildew is usually a cosmetic problem only and can be removed with a bleach solution or shake cleaner. Moss can also be removed.

Water damage often does not appear in the obvious form of dripping water inside living areas. Often the water slowly seeps into the drywall or plaster, causing discoloration. Water stains in the attic are often a sign of bigger problems to come.

Loose or missing counterflashing (which attaches to the brick or wall) can usually be reattached using roofing cement. Gaps between flashing pieces can also be sealed with cement. A hole or small area of rust can also be repaired (see pages 92–93). If rust is general the flashing should be replaced. If the area has been leaking for some time, call in a pro.

Where shingles rest on top of metal flashing, they usually need to be sealed tightly onto the flashing. Often they can be resealed using roofing cement in a caulking-gun tube or by using a trowel.

SPOT AND EMERGENCY REPAIRS

The source of a leak typically is not directly above where water appears. Once a leak shows up in an attic or stains an interior ceiling, it has probably traveled several feet or more along a rafter or joist. That means you will need to do some investigation to discover the source of the leak. A trip into the attic with a flashlight is the first step.

Of course leaks are easiest to locate during or immediately after a heavy rain. Often, however, trickling water leaves a stain that can be spotted after it has dried.

These pages show quick solutions that will protect your ceilings and walls at least temporarily. For longer-lasting fixes see pages 88–95.

PRESTART CHECKLIST

☐ **TIME**
Most leaks take less than 2 hours to diagnose and temporarily repair, but some leaks can require several attempts before the solution is found.

☐ **TOOLS**
Flashlight, tape measure, screwdriver, trowel, caulking gun, hammer, flat pry bar, drill

☐ **SKILLS**
Measuring, cutting, fastening

☐ **PREP**
Make preparations for working safely on the roof (pages 22–25).

☐ **MATERIALS**
Roofing cement (in a caulk tube or a can), plastic sheeting, plywood, buckets

Locating a leak

1 In the attic find the source of the leak and measure up to the peak or down to the eave. Also measure over to the nearest rake. As an alternative you may be able to poke a wire through the hole where water is coming through.

2 Go on the roof and measure down from the reference points you have chosen. Take into account the rake overhang or any other differences from the inside measurements.

STANLEY PRO TIP: **Removing and driving hidden nails**

Repairs often call for removing or driving nails that rest below a shingle. Work on a warm day, when the shingles are not brittle, and lift up shingle tabs. Tap a flat pry bar under the nailhead and use a scrap of lumber to protect the roofing as you pry it up. If the nail is long, you may need to use pliers to complete the removal.

To drive a hidden nail, use the same tools, place the flat part of the pry bar over the nailhead, and pound on the bar to drive the nail.

Temporary solutions

Water that drips down a board may change its course eventually. To ensure a reliable path, attach a wood scrap to a rafter to divert the stream downward. Place a bucket below to catch the water before it can do any damage.

A sheet of plywood can temporarily protect a large area, although it won't completely seal out all the water. Pressure-treated plywood will last longest; OSB will start to flake apart after one rainstorm. If possible extend the plywood past the peak so that water will be less likely to seep under. Attach it with screws or nails.

For additional protection cover the plywood with plastic sheeting. Screw or nail strips of 1×2 or lath at the edges.

Spot repairs

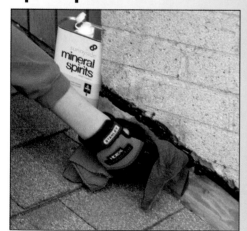

Where flashing has come apart from a wall or another piece of flashing, press the flashing back into place—you may need to use a block or other heavy weight to hold it in place—and apply roofing cement with a caulk tube. To ensure that water won't seep behind the flashing, smooth the cement with a rag that's been soaked in mineral spirits.

Shingles may come loose and even curl up near a valley, rake, or eave. Lift up the tab, spread roofing cement on the drip edge or starter strip, and press the tab back in place.

If a shingle tab has broken and you can find the missing part, glue it back into place with roofing cement and smear some cement over the crack. If you cannot find the missing part, or if you want a better-looking repair, replace the shingle (page 88).

REPLACING SHINGLES AND SHAKES

You may have some composition shingles in your garage or shed left over from the original roofing job. If not take along a sample shingle when you buy replacements so that you can match the color. Replacement wood shakes or shingles will be lighter in color than the rest of the roof, but they will darken in time.

If the felt underlayment is damaged, cut a piece that is at least 6 inches larger than the damaged area in both directions and slip it into place before replacing the shingle or shake. Sound underlayment is especially important on a wood shake or shingle roof. If you are making repairs at the eaves, you may need to replace a starter strip or starter shingles (see pages 45–46).

PRESTART CHECKLIST

☐ **TIME**
Once you have the repair materials, an hour or less for most repairs

☐ **TOOLS**
Utility knife, tape measure, flat pry bar, stapler, hammer or roofing hatchet, trowel, caulk gun, nail set

☐ **SKILLS**
Nailing; using a pry bar, chisel, caulk gun

☐ **PREP**
Buy replacement shingles or shakes to match and make preparations for working safely on the roof (pages 22–25).

☐ **MATERIALS**
Shingles or shakes, roofing cement (in a caulk tube or a can), nails long enough to penetrate the sheathing

Replacing shingles

1 On a warm (but not hot) day, lift up the tabs of the shingles above the damaged shingle or shingles. Use a flat pry bar to pry out the nails. Pull out the damaged shingles and clear away any debris.

2 If the underlayment is incomplete or torn, patch over it. Cut a piece that is about 6 inches larger than the damaged area in both directions and slip it in under the surrounding shingles. Drive a couple of staples to hold it in place.

3 Starting at the bottom and working up, install the replacement shingles (see page 47). You will have to lift up shingle tabs to drive some of the nails.

4 Before installing the topmost piece, apply a bead of roofing cement to its underside, near the top. Slip the shingle into place, lift up the tabs above, and drive nails.

Replacing wood shakes or shingles

1 Use a hammer and chisel to split apart the damaged shake along its grain.

2 You may be able to pull out the parts with your hands. If not use a hammer and chisel to force the parts down and out. Pull out or drive down any hidden nails.

3 Reassemble the damaged shake and use it as a template for cutting the replacement. Score the new piece several times with a knife and snap the pieces apart. Or cut with a circular saw.

4 Position the replacement shake about 1 inch below the shakes on either side. There should be a ¼- to ⅜-inch gap on either side. Drive two shake nails at angles. You may choose to use a nail set to finish driving them flush; do not set the heads below the wood surface.

5 Use a hammer and a scrap of wood to drive the shake up into position, aligned with the shakes on either side.

STANLEY PRO TIP

Cleaning and sealing shakes

A wood shake or shingle roof can be cleaned using a wood-bleach solution or a product made specifically for cedar roofs. Apply with a pump sprayer, brush with a stiff broom, and rinse thoroughly with water. For heavy-duty cleaning you can use a power washer, but use one that does not have high pressure and work carefully. Cedar is a soft wood and can be damaged by a high-pressure spray.

Preservatives and sealers can also be applied with a pump sprayer. Consult with a local dealer for the type of sealer best suited to your area.

REPAIRS TO A FLAT ROOF

A flat roof is usually slightly sloped. It may be covered with a granular roll roofing, EPDM (which is smooth surfaced), or modified bitumen (which may be smooth or mineral surfaced); see pages 74–81. Some flat roofs have hot tar built-up roofing, which may have a gravel surface. If you live in an arid region or an older urban area, you may have a large flat roof. Suburban homes sometimes have small flat sections.

Where the roofing curves to meet a wall or chimney, the material may loosen along its topmost edges. Apply plenty of roofing cement to fill the void and smooth the cement so water can run off unimpeded.

An application of aluminum fiber coating quickly seals many small leaks and can prolong the life of a roof. It cannot be applied over a gravel-topped or mineral surfaced roof however.

PRESTART CHECKLIST

☐ **TIME**
1 to 2 hours for most repairs

☐ **TOOLS**
Utility knife, trowel, squeegee/broom for applying aluminum coating, hammer

☐ **SKILLS**
No special skills required

☐ **PREP**
Inspect the roof for bubbles, cracks, and voids.

☐ **MATERIALS**
Roofing cement, fiber-mesh patching, EPDM or other flat-roofing material, roofing nails

Patching a small hole or bubble

1 Use a utility knife to cut a slit in a bubble or lift up the two sides of a crack. You may need to cut out a narrow strip so the two sides can lie flat. Use a trowel to slip some roofing cement under the damaged area.

2 Spread roofing cement over an area that is 6 or more inches wider than the damage. Embed fiberglass mesh in the cement, then apply another layer of cement. Use a trowel to feather the edges.

Applying aluminum coating

An aluminum coating can be applied over a hot-tar roof or an EPDM roof. It not only seals cracks but also reflects light, making the roof somewhat cooler in the summer. Apply it over the entire roof with a squeegee/broom tool.

STANLEY PRO TIP

Dealing with bubbles and blisters

Small blisters often appear on a hot-tar roof. If they fill with water and freeze in the winter, cracks can result. The broken blisters can be filled in with roofing cement or with aluminum-fiber coating.

Bubbles under the surface can be felt when you walk on the roof. Sometimes they even fill with water. Air-filled bubbles may not be an immediate problem, but they can open up and cause leaks. It is best to slit them, let out the air or water, and glue down the area.

Patching a larger area

1 Use a utility knife and straightedge to cut a rectangle around the damage. Cut just deep enough that you can remove the piece. Use the piece as a template to cut a patch.

2 Spread roofing cement onto the cutout area and work it under the surrounding roofing as well. Set the patch into the wet cement.

3 Cut a patch that is about 6 inches longer and wider than the first patch. Spread roofing cement, set the patch into the cement, and spread another layer of cement over the patch. Once it has dried coat the area with aluminum-fiber coating.

STANLEY PRO TIP: **Tile roof repairs**

If you have broken clay tiles, call in a roofer for evaluation. If the tiles are weakening and growing brittle with age, you may need to reroof. Walk on a tile roof only if you are certain that the tiles can bear your weight. Otherwise you risk cracking tiles.

If your roof has mortared joints at the ridge and elsewhere, the mortar may develop cracks. If the cracks are small, caulk them using a mortar-type caulk that comes close to matching the mortar's color. Otherwise replace the mortar following these steps.

1 Use a narrow cold chisel and hammer to gently chip out the damaged mortar. In most cases the ridge tiles will come loose when you do this.

2 Mix a batch of Type S mortar; make it stiff enough that it will not flow. Apply the mortar to the ridge gap. Soak the ridge tiles in water and set them into the mortar. Use a trowel to smooth the mortar and seal it against the field and ridge tiles.

FLASHING REPAIRS

Flashing is the final line of defense against water infiltration, protecting a roof at vulnerable joints between the roof and vertical surfaces.

Often the flashing itself is not the problem; the roofing cement or caulk that secures the flashing may have cracks or gaps. Fill these gaps completely (see page 87).

If the flashing sealed well once but no longer does because of a gap or rusted area, you can use the old flashing as a template and install new flashing exactly the same way as the old. However if flashing was installed incorrectly to begin with—if valley flashing was nailed near the center or if flashing around a chimney was incorrectly configured—you should call in a professional to install new flashing correctly.

If drip-edge flashing fails, the fascia along the eaves or the rake could be damaged. See pages 176–177 for how to repair fascia and soffits.

Eaves and rake flashing

1 If drip-edge flashing allows water to seep behind, it can damage the fascia. Pry up the starter strip and the first course of shingles and pry out the nails holding the drip edge.

2 Cut new pieces to fit tightly at corners (see page 43). Attach the new pieces with nails or screws.

PRESTART CHECKLIST

☐ **TIME**
An hour or so for most flashing repairs

☐ **TOOLS**
Trowel, caulking gun, hammer, flat pry bar, wire brush, drill

☐ **SKILLS**
Basic carpentry skills

☐ **PREP**
Make preparations for working safely on or next to the roof (pages 22–25).

☐ **MATERIALS**
Replacement flashings, sheet metal, roofing cement (in a caulk tube or a can), nails, screws

Spot repairs

Fill small holes with roofing cement or gutter caulk. For a large area wire-brush away all rust and debris. Cut a piece of sheet metal several inches larger than the damaged area. Apply roofing cement or gutter caulk and embed the metal. Use a trowel or a damp rag to feather the edges of the cement.

STANLEY PRO TIP

Use the right materials

Some flashings are made of galvanized steel, which often rusts when the galvanizing wears off. Many newer flashings are made of aluminum, which never rusts. Plastic flashings are similarly rust-resistant and are gaining acceptance as they prove themselves durable over the long term.

Copper flashing is durable and has a classic look. In time it will turn a subtle shade of green. Be sure to use copper nails; other metals can cause corrosion.

Lead, or lead-coated copper, is often used for a tile or slate roof. It is expensive, but it molds easily around irregular shapes.

Vent flashing

1 To pull out a boot flashing, you will need to cut through some roofing cement and lift up shingle tabs on each side and at the top. Have replacement roofing on hand; you'll likely damage the shingles.

2 Buy a new boot flashing to fit over the pipe, slip it partway down, then lift the upper shingles so you can slip under the flashing flange. Seal the underside of the flange with roofing cement.

3 Drive nails to attach it. Notch the shingle to be applied over the flashing. Apply cement to the undersides of the upper and side shingles where they rest on top of the flange.

Valley flashing

1 Where valley flashing is damaged or where a seam is coming loose, wire-brush the area and apply roofing cement. Smooth it with a putty knife or trowel.

2 Feather the edges of the cement so water can flow easily, then embed fiberglass mesh in the cement.

3 Paint the patch with aluminum coating to cover the roofing cement. Or wait for the cement to dry completely and apply acrylic or oil-base paint to match the flashing.

CHIMNEY REPAIRS

More than any other part of a house, a brick chimney is exposed to the heat of the sun, driving rain, and freeze-thaw cycles. No wonder, then, that chimney mortar joints often develop gaps, and the brick faces sometimes start to crumble—a condition known as spalling. If the chimney top is made of masonry, cracks are almost certain to develop.

Easy repairs made at an early stage will save work in the long run. Simply painting on masonry sealer (see Pro Tip on page 95) can save you plenty of work in the future.

PRESTART CHECKLIST

☐ **TIME**
Several hours to repoint a chimney; an hour or less for other repairs

☐ **TOOLS**
Trowels, grinder or joint-raking tool, pointing tool, masonry brush, flat pry bar, hammer, caulking gun

☐ **SKILLS**
Cutting sheet metal, working with mortar

☐ **PREP**
Make preparations for working safely on the roof (pages 22–25).

☐ **MATERIALS**
Mortar mix, perhaps masonry colorant, roofing cement (in a caulk tube or a can), exterior caulk, scraps of plywood, bucket, masonry sealer, latex bonding agent

Chimney flashing

Chimneys have a variety of specifically shaped pieces (see pages 52–53). To remove a piece of flashing you will likely need to bend up some counterflashing, remove a shingle or two, and remove other flashing pieces.

If counterflashing has partially come out of the mortar joint, gently pull it all the way out. Squirt some exterior caulk or roofing cement into the joint and press the counterflashing back in. If that doesn't work you may need to chip out the mortar, repoint the joint (see the next page), and press the counterflashing into the new mortar.

Chimney caps

If a corner has broken off, make a simple L-shape form by screwing together two pieces of plywood. Use duct tape to hold the form tight against the cap. Paint the broken area with liquid latex bonding agent. Mix a batch of Type S mortar, pour it into the form, and smooth with a wood or magnesium float.

Seal cracks, as well as gaps between the chimney and the flue, using exterior mortar caulk or roofing cement.

Repointing

1 Remove all mortar to a depth of at least ½ inch. This is easiest to do using a grinder equipped with a masonry blade, but you can also use a hand raking tool or a small chisel and hammer.

2 In a bucket mix a batch of repointing mortar. You may choose to add colorant to approximate an existing mortar color. Wet the joints that are to be filled.

3 Place some mortar on a large trowel or a piece of plywood and press it against the wall just below the empty joint. Use a pointing tool to press the mortar into the joint. Fill the horizontal joints first, then the verticals.

4 Use a masonry brush to smooth the joints so they are roughly flush with the bricks.

WHAT IF...
You want a more finished look?

Because a chimney is usually far from view, brushed joints are usually fine. If you want neater-looking joints, use a jointer tool designed to make your type of joint; a concave jointer is the most common. As soon as the mortar is stiff enough to hold a thumbprint, use the jointer to smooth the horizontal joints, then the verticals.

STANLEY PRO TIP

Sealing bricks

You can protect brick and other masonry surfaces by simply applying liquid masonry sealer. Use a fairly stiff masonry brush to work the sealer into all the joints and pores.

If the brick surfaces are starting to crumble and the appearance of the chimney is not important, consider applying a skim coat of mortar over the entire brick surface. First wire-brush away all loose material, then paint with latex bonding agent. Mix a stiff batch of mortar, apply it with a trowel, and smooth it with a masonry brush.

VENTING AN ATTIC

A well-ventilated attic will maintain a temperature near that of the air outside. During the winter, cold attic air prevents ice damming (see page 84). In the winter a well-ventilated attic will often have a thick blanket of unmelted snow on its roof, while a nearby roof of the same pitch with inadequate ventilation will display bare spots. Of course thick attic-floor insulation also helps keep the attic from heating up. In the summer proper ventilation keeps an attic from overheating, which can cause serious damage, especially if the hot air is humid. Poorly ventilated attics can reach temperatures of 150°F.

Homes built prior to the 1980s were often built with what is today considered inadequate ventilation. If you have an older home, it may make sense to upgrade the ventilation when you reshingle the roof.

Ventilation means flow-through of air. In a typical arrangement air flows up through soffit vents under the eaves and out through a ridge vent at the peak or through roof vents near the peak. Some older homes have a cupola vent on the roof's peak. In another arrangement gable vents located near the peaks of rake ends pull air through the attic.

Of course air must flow freely. If a soffit vent gets clogged with insulation, it will not distribute air. Some turbine-style roof vents spin with the upflow of warm air flowing through them; if the spinning mechanism

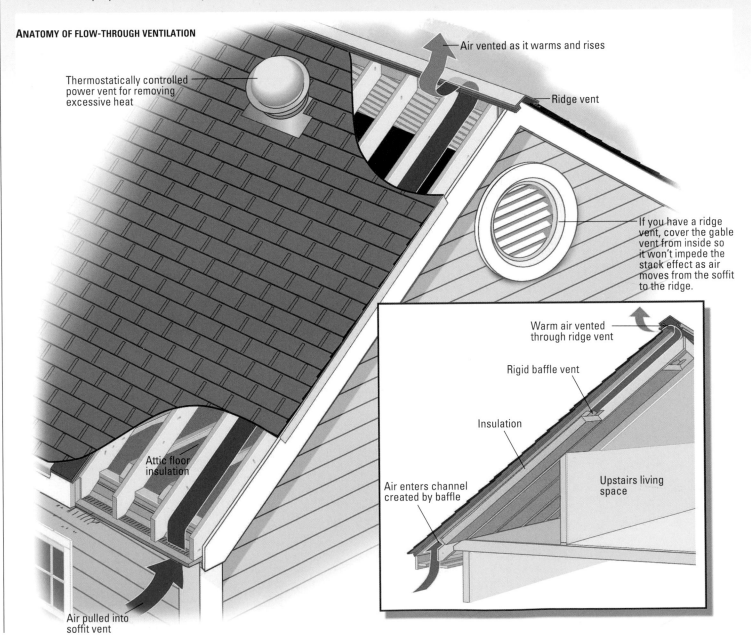

ANATOMY OF FLOW-THROUGH VENTILATION

Thermostatically controlled power vent for removing excessive heat

Air vented as it warms and rises

Ridge vent

If you have a ridge vent, cover the gable vent from inside so it won't impede the stack effect as air moves from the soffit to the ridge.

Attic floor insulation

Air pulled into soffit vent

Warm air vented through ridge vent

Rigid baffle vent

Insulation

Upstairs living space

Air enters channel created by baffle

gets stuck, they will be less efficient.

Check with your building department or roofing supplier to find out how much ventilation is considered adequate in your locale. Typically if your attic floor insulation has a vapor barrier (look between floor joists for plastic sheeting covering the ceiling below), you should have 1 square foot of soffit vent opening and 1 square foot of ridge or roof vent opening for every 300 square feet of attic floor area. If the insulation is blown in, with no vapor barrier, double

the ventilation to 1 square foot for every 150 square attic feet. In a finished attic with insulation pushed against the sheathing, you may need to add **rigid baffles** to allow air to move behind the insulation (inset, page 96).

For a **roof vent** you can choose either **ridge vents (roll-type** or **rigid)** that are covered by ridge roofing or those that have a visible metal cap. Roof vents may be square **cap roof vents (skylight** types help illumine the attic) or they may be **turbines.**

Gable vents have louvers to keep out most

of the rain; they may not be a good idea on a wall that receives driving rain. **Power vents,** for either the roof or a gable, add extra venting power when the attic heats up. Some are **solar-powered,** sparing you the chore of running power to the unit.

Under-the-soffit vents include individual **rectangular** or **circular vents,** and a long **continuous vent.**

The four pages that follow show how to install most of these products.

VENT OPTIONS

Roll-type ridge vent

Rigid-type ridge vent

Rigid baffle

Continuous soffit vent

Cap roof vent

Solar-powered power vent

Turbine

Skylight roof vent

Gable vent

Rectangular and circular soffit vents

INSTALLING ATTIC VENTS

Ridge and roof vents are easier to install just prior to a roofing job, but they can also be retrofitted onto an existing roof. Soffit vents can be installed anytime.

Venting goes hand in hand with insulation. Measure the thickness of your attic floor insulation (or wall and ceiling insulation, if the attic is finished) and ask your building department or a home center whether you should add more.

If you need more ventilation but don't want to cut a new hole in the roof or gable, consider adding a power vent, which can be controlled by a thermostat and/or a wall switch.

PRESTART CHECKLIST

☐ **TIME**
Several hours to install most venting products

☐ **TOOLS**
Tape measure, drill, reciprocating saw, jigsaw, chalkline, circular saw, hammer and chisel, trowel

☐ **SKILLS**
Basic carpentry and roofing

☐ **PREP**
Determine how much and what type of ventilation you need. Tear off the roofing or plan to cut back shingles for the installations. Make preparations for working safely on the roof (pages 22–25).

☐ **MATERIALS**
Soffit, roof, ridge, or gable vents; nails and screws; roofing; roofing cement

Soffit vents

1 Position soffit vents, whether rectangular or circular, about midway between joists. You can often locate joists by looking for nailheads on the soffit or by using a stud finder.

2 Make a cardboard template for the openings, which should be about 2 inches shorter and narrower than the vents; make sure you will have room for driving the mounting screws. Drill a hole or two inside the lines, insert the blade of a reciprocating saw (shown) or jigsaw, and cut the opening.

3 Inside the attic make sure air can flow freely through the vents. If you have blown-in insulation, you may need to cut and attach blocking to keep the insulation from blocking the vent.

4 Position the vent over the opening and drive the mounting screws. Use stainless-steel screws, which won't rust.

Ridge vents

1 Snap chalklines on both sides of the ridge to cut a slot of the recommended size—typically 1½ inches on each side of the peak. Set a circular saw blade to cut through the sheathing, without damaging the rafters below. Stop cutting about 12 inches from the end of the ridge or as recommended by the manufacturer. Finish the cut with a hammer and chisel.

2 Add roofing up to the hole cut for the vent. The venting may come in pieces or a continuous strip. If using a continuous strip, cut it into two pieces and work from each end to the middle, taking care to keep the pieces fairly taut so they don't sag.

3 Drive nails through the holes provided or every 12 inches, making sure nails penetrate the sheathing.

4 With this type of vent, the underside must be cut away so the vent seals at the end. Other vents have end caps at the rake. Make sure the vent seals against the roof on each side.

5 Cut ridgecaps as you would for a standard roof (page 49). Set each so it wraps the ridge vent. Use a 5-inch reveal on the ridgecap.

6 Use long roofing nails—2-inchers often will do the job—that completely penetrate the sheathing. Drive the nails just flush, without indenting them.

Other ridge vents

Gable vents can actually interfere with the airflow through a ridge vent because they reduce the chimney effect; manufacturers recommend covering them from the inside.

Some ridge vents are made of a thick mesh that resembles a scrubbing pad (see page 97); roll it out, pull taut, drive nails, and then apply the hip shingles.

Roof vents

1 To install a roof vent onto existing roofing, drill a locator hole from the inside of the attic to ensure that you will not cut through a joist. Mark the roof with the manufacturer's template and cut the hole with a reciprocating saw.

2 Pry up the shingles surrounding the upper half of the hole and pull out nails as needed. You may need to cut back some shingles. Slide the vent into place so that the top half of its flange is covered with shingles.

3 Drive roofing nails and cover them with roofing cement. Use roofing cement to seal down the roofing above and below the vent.

INSTALLING A ROOF FAN

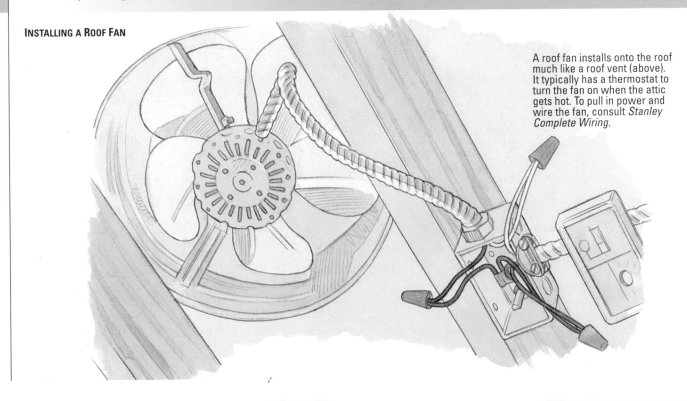

A roof fan installs onto the roof much like a roof vent (above). It typically has a thermostat to turn the fan on when the attic gets hot. To pull in power and wire the fan, consult *Stanley Complete Wiring*.

Gable vents

1 Cut a hole that will be covered by the vent frame. Set a circular saw to cut just deep enough through the siding and sheathing. Or use a jigsaw and stop when you come to a stud.

2 Attach the vent louver panel by driving screws into the siding and sheathing. Caulk the edges as needed.

3 You may need to modify the framing, depending on whether the gable framing is 16 or 24 inches on center. If installing a gable fan (see below), add top and bottom horizontal framing.

Gable fan

 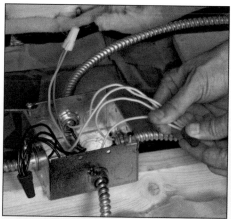 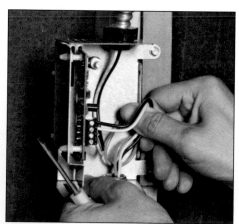

1 Mount a gable fan by driving screws through the mounting flanges into framing members.

2 **Shut off power to the circuit** and run code-approved cable to a nearby junction box. If no junction box is available in the attic, bring power up from a circuit in the room below. See *Stanley Complete Wiring* for wiring instructions.

3 Wire the thermostat following the manufacturer's directions. With the thermostat shown, stripped wire ends are inserted in a terminal bar and screwed tight. Adjust the thermostat control and restore power.

PREPARING FOR SIDING

This chapter will help you choose the right siding for your house from the many materials available. It will also show you the essentials of applying siding, including the all-important jobs of installing flashing and trim—two key elements that can make or break any siding job.

Siding is usually less daunting work than roofing. You will need ladders and perhaps scaffolding for upper floors, but the logistics of working on the side of a house are simpler than those for working on a roof. It pays to plan and work carefully; many of the safety tips on pages 22–25 apply.

Correctly installed siding goes a long way toward protecting your home from moisture. However in recent years it has become apparent that a simple layer of roofing felt or building paper may not be adequate to keep out all the wet, especially in vulnerable areas such as those around windows and doors, at the bottom of the sheathing, and at corners. In addition to infiltration from rain and snow, many newer homes have moisture problems arising from tightly sealed walls that cannot breathe properly.

Close attention to flashing and trim eases siding installation and protects your home from the weather. This chapter shows you how to install a variety of flashings to add extra protection. If there is a chance of moisture being trapped between the siding and the house, consider a rain-screen installation (page 143). Consult with local suppliers, builders, and building inspectors to determine the type of flashings needed for your climate.

If you plan to install new windows and doors, it usually—but not always—makes sense to repair the sheathing, apply building paper or felt, and then install the windows or doors prior to the siding. This chapter gives some tips on window and door installation, but you should consult a book such as *Stanley Complete Doors & Windows* for more detailed information. If your soffits, fascia, or gutters need repairing or replacing, do the work before or while you install the siding; see pages 176–185.

Close attention to flashing and trim protects your home from the weather.

CHAPTER PREVIEW

Understanding siding and framing
page 104

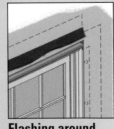
Flashing around windows and doors
page 105

Choosing siding materials
page 106

Removing siding and repairing sheathing
page 110

The layered look
New flashing materials and methods help eliminate moisture incursion and eventual damage to siding. They may seem a bit complicated but are based on the principle of stair-stepping layers that force water to flow off—not into—the structure.

Adhesive flashing, like the water-shedding tape shown above, seals the opening for a new window. Similar flashing should be applied around doors and to inside and outside corners.

Applying felt or building paper
page 112

Applying trim
page 114

UNDERSTANDING SIDING AND FRAMING

Before you order siding materials, be sure you understand how your walls are put together. Most homes have 2×4 or 2×6 studs (which are 1½ inches thick) positioned 16 inches "on center," meaning 16 inches from the center of one stud to the center of the next stud. Some homes are built with studs on 24-inch centers. However, the spacing between the wall's corner and the next-to-last stud will usually be a shorter distance. At windows and doors there will be additional framing members, but if the framing has been done correctly they will not interfere with the regular on-center spacing that runs throughout the wall.

Be aware, however, that framing is not always installed correctly, especially in older homes, where stud spacing may be irregular. And some studs may be installed out of plumb. If your siding is installed with nails driven into studs (rather than into sheathing), it pays to spend a little extra time confirming the location of every stud.

It is important to know what sort of sheathing you have. If it is solid plywood or OSB, some types of siding can be fastened to it. However, if the sheathing is made of a fibrous material, gypsum, foam insulation, or other soft material, it is not firm enough to hold a nail and you must install the siding with nails driven into the studs. In this case, you must also position any joints in the centers of studs; adjoining pieces can be attached to the same stud.

The sheathing should be protected with house wrap (which is generally light in color), building paper, or roofing felt. These products have undergone improvements over the years, making them more resistant to moisture while still allowing the house to breathe. See pages 112–113 for information on applying these materials.

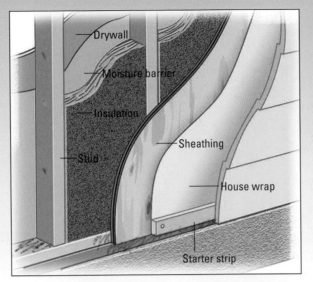

Drywall
Moisture barrier
Insulation
Sheathing
Stud
House wrap
Starter strip

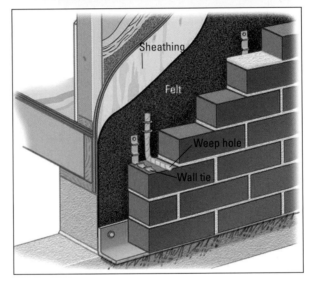

Sheathing
Felt
Weep hole
Wall tie

Horizontal siding may be beveled, in shingle form, or tongue-and-groove. It may be made of wood, fiber cement, or pressed wood. If the sheathing is solid plywood or OSB, you may be able to attach it to the sheathing. In most cases, however, nails should be driven into the studs. At the bottom of the installation, a wood strip, additional layer of siding, or special starter strip makes the bottom piece flare out a bit more.

Brick or stone veneer is held together using mortar joints. Metal wall ties placed at regular intervals secure the wall to the sheathing. Small ropes placed near the bottom make a "weep hole" where moisture can exit, thereby protecting the sheathing from wet rot.

Balloon framing

Most homes are built with platform framing, meaning there is a single or double horizontal 2× member at the bottom and the top of each floor. In addition there is usually a wide rim joist providing a solid nailing surface between each floor. An old home may be built with balloon framing, in which case there are no plates or rim joists.

FLASHING AROUND WINDOWS AND DOORS

In many areas it is acceptable to simply install building wrap and pieces of drip-cap flashing over the top of windows and doors. However, manufacturers and building codes often call for more elaborate flashings to protect the sheathing, studs, and interior walls. Whether you are installing new windows and doors or siding to existing units, plan and carefully install flashings that meet local codes and provide maximum protection against moisture.

The general principle is: As any moisture (which may collect due to condensation or small gaps in the siding) flows downward, it should not have an opportunity to infiltrate behind the house wrap where it can do damage. So the upper piece of wrap or flashing should go over any lower pieces.

The type and location of the flashings will vary depending on the type of windows and doors. If you have vinyl- or metal-flanged windows, for instance, you may install drip-cap flashing over the window itself or over the top trim piece that you install. For a wood unit, drip-cap flashing may be installed over the trim piece (often called brick molding) that comes with the window or door. Consult manufacturer's instructions for the recommended technique.

In addition to metal flashing, self-adhesive flashings, similar to WSU sheets used for roofing edges (see pages 40–41), are often applied around window or door openings. If you are installing a new unit, the self-adhesive flashing will cover the inside of the framing as well as the sheathing. If the window already exists, the self-adhesive flashing will likely cover the sheathing and any window flanges only. In addition, self-adhesive flashing is sometimes installed at wall corners where it can be attached over the building wrap. Consult manufacturer's instructions, your local building department, or a professional siding installer who works in your area.

When installing a window in new construction (right), the building wrap overlaps the self-adhesive flashing. In a remodeling job, a simpler arrangement is often used: Self-adhesive flashing strips are applied along the bottom, then the sides, then the top. Then small pieces of flashing are applied over the gaps at the corners.

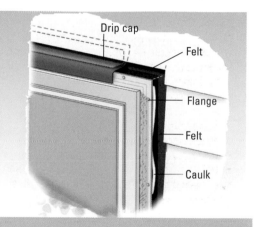

In this arrangement, felt or building paper is first stapled to the sheathing, with the top pieces overlapping the lower pieces. A bead of caulk is applied to the felt and the window is set in the caulk. Next comes another layer of building wrap, installed like the first layer. At the top, metal drip-cap flashing is tucked up under the siding and on top of the second layer of wrap and the trim is installed just under the drip cap.

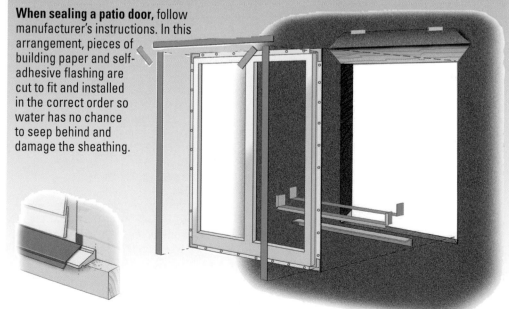

When sealing a patio door, follow manufacturer's instructions. In this arrangement, pieces of building paper and self-adhesive flashing are cut to fit and installed in the correct order so water has no chance to seep behind and damage the sheathing.

CHOOSING SIDING MATERIALS

Any type of siding sold at a home center will do the basic job of sealing out weather, as long as it is installed correctly. Some require more maintenance than others. Only vinyl and metal sidings are truly impervious to water, but they must be installed carefully in order to protect the sheathing underneath. Solid wood and fiber-cement products are resistant to moisture but need to be protected with paint or sealer and should not contact standing water. Plywood and hardboard products are quickly damaged if they get wet.

Lap siding

Individual horizontal siding strips that overlap each other are often called clapboards. Cedar is a popular (though pricey) choice because it is naturally insulating, stable, and easy to work with. It has some natural preservatives but will rot if exposed to moisture for long periods; the lighter-colored sapwood is more susceptible than the darker heartwood. Beveled cedar clapboards come in various grades. Widths range from 4 to 12 inches;

6-inch-wide boards are the most common size. The term "beveled" refers to the fact that the boards are wider at the bottom end than the top. Better boards are knot-free ("clear") or have only tiny knots. Clapboards with vertical grain (evidenced by closely spaced and fairly straight grain lines) may be called "quartersawn" and are less likely to warp and shrink than boards with flat grain (evidenced by widely spaced and wavy grain lines). To ensure against rot, order primed or prestained cedar.

Channeled and beveled cedar has a lip (inset) that slips over the piece below, simplifying installation. The channels make the boards more stable. You may also choose cedar-beveled siding with decorative edges.

Preprimed wood siding may be made of Scandinavian pine or another light-colored wood. The wood itself is not as rot-resistant as cedar, but the priming is a great help.

Fiber-cement lap siding comes in various widths and is usually not beveled. Some types are smooth; others have a wood-grain texture. This material is inexpensive and easy to work with. Once installed and painted, it is difficult to distinguish from wood siding. It resists cracking but will swell if exposed to moisture for prolonged periods.

Primed hardboard and textured OSB (oriented-strand board) are the least expensive options. They are also easy to work with and will last a long time if kept well sealed with paint. However, if a bare surface is exposed to moisture, it will swell quickly.

Panel siding

The quickest way to side a house is to install panel siding, also called sheet siding. The sides have shiplap edges so that one piece laps onto its neighbor. The most common panel size is 4 by 8 feet, but sheets 10 and 12 feet long are also available and are worth the extra weight if they eliminate horizontal butt joints.

Rough-sawn plywood, called Texture 1-11 (or T1-11), has been a popular siding option for many years. However, this product can buckle, warp, or even come apart if it is not

installed correctly and kept well sealed. The cheapest types must be sealed with primer and two or more coats of exterior paint and attached with nails every 16 inches. Higher-end products are thicker, use better wood and glue, and come with a first coat of sealer. Stain-grade panels have no football-shape patches. See page 147 for more information on choosing panel siding. Typically these panels have vertical grooves (the panels should be installed upright, so water will not sit in the grooves). The grooves may be evenly or variably spaced.

Smooth-sided panels are often used to create a faux board-and-batten look (see page 150). Alternatively the joint between panels can be covered by a single batten.

You can also buy **fiber-cement panels,** made of the same material as fiber-cement lap siding. A preprimed panel will save you time since the backs of these panels should be painted before installing.

At the lowest end, **pressed hardboard and OSB panels** come with embossed surfaces that are covered with a thin coating that is somewhat hard. These materials need to be completely sealed with several coats of paint at all points or they will soak up water like a sponge.

Tongue-and-groove or lapped horizontal siding

This type of siding is available in wood only. Car siding fits together in a shiplap arrangement, with the top piece lapping over the lower piece. Cedar tongue-and-groove, or drop, siding may have a decorative curved surface at the top (see page 128 for several joint types). Installation is easier than for standard lap siding because you can simply stack them on top of each other without measuring the exposure.

Vinyl siding

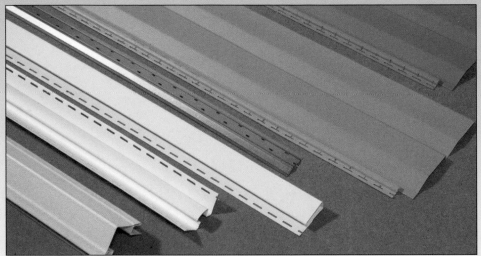

In most areas of the country, **vinyl** is the most popular material for re-siding a house. It installs quickly, requires little maintenance, and is inexpensive. A wealth of colors and styles is available. Insulated vinyl siding was once popular but is no longer, because it contributes to moisture problems and provides little actual insulation. Buy all the various trim pieces—outside corners, window and door trims—at the same time as the siding itself. Make sure they will fit well against your home's windows and doors (you may leave existing trim in place or remove it).

Vinyl siding is installed horizontally and looks like clapboard. The most common type is called D5, meaning each piece has two courses with 5-inch exposures. Other configurations include T3 siding, which has three 3-inch-wide courses.

Aluminum and steel siding

Metal sidings are available in clapboard-look panels like vinyl siding, but you can also buy vertical siding with a board-and-batten look. **Aluminum siding** is less common than it used to be but is still popular in some areas. It is durable but needs to be painted often. It is more likely to get dented, in which case you will have to repair it with autobody filler. Newer types of **steel siding** (shown above) are top-coated with a colored PVC finish that is very durable and resistant to denting. It is pricey however. Steel may be recommended in areas with high winds, which can tear off lighter vinyl and aluminum sidings.

Cedar shingles

Smooth-sided shingles are the usual choice for siding, though **cedar shakes** (see page 56) are often used. Western red cedar is the most common wood species. The No. 1 grade shingles are dark heartwood (for greater rot resistance), have closely spaced vertical grain, and are clear of any knots; No. 2 shingles have some light-colored sapwood (which hardly resists rot at all), some vertical and some widely spaced flat grain, and some knots; and No. 3 shingles have plenty of sapwood, flat grain, and knots and are useful only as a starter course. Choose the highest grade you can afford. You can also buy cedar shingles already assembled onto plywood or OSB panels (see page 142). They install quickly but are expensive.

Stucco

A masonry product applied directly to a wall, stucco is durable and beautiful if installed well. Two or three coats of stucco are used to create a thick surface that resists cracking. The stucco may be tinted for long-lasting color or it can be painted over. A variety of stucco textures can be applied (see page 173), some of which reflect the personality of the worker.

Masonry siding

A new generation of stone-look products made of durable cast concrete can be applied directly to an exterior wall of a house. Some of these imitate cobblestone, while others give the appearance of neatly stacked stones. Once attached to the house, the joints must be neatly filled with mortar.

Faux shakes and masonry

If you want the look of painted cedar shakes or masonry without the difficult installation, consider vinyl or fiber-cement panels molded in a wide variety of shapes, textures, and colors. These install quickly and require no special skills (see page 141). Vinyl panels require almost no maintenance; fiber-cement panels need to be painted.

REMOVING SIDING AND REPAIRING SHEATHING

Before installing new siding you will need to remove some of the old siding. Before you start determine which wood pieces will stay and take care not to damage them while removing siding. A flat pry bar and hammer will take care of most of the job, but special tools can help speed up the removal.

Have a plan for disposing of the old siding. Unless the area to be stripped is small, you will probably want to rent a roll-off trash container. Arrange to have it delivered as close to the site as possible and create plank paths for wheelbarrows so you can fill the bin without damaging your yard. Place drop cloths or plastic sheeting on the ground to minimize cleanup later (see page 20).

Plan to cover the bare sheathing with building wrap on the same day that you remove the old siding.

PRESTART CHECKLIST

☐ **TIME**
Working with one or two helpers, a day to remove 1,600 square feet or so of siding; sheathing repairs vary.

☐ **TOOLS**
Hammer, flat pry bar, cat's paw nail remover, roofer's shovel, release magnet for picking up nails, drill, reciprocating saw, ladders or scaffolding

☐ **SKILLS**
Basic carpentry skills

☐ **PREP**
Protect your yard and plantings and make pathways for delivering the old siding to adisposal container.

☐ **MATERIALS**
Drop cloths or plastic sheeting, lumber to repair sheathing

Removing siding and trim

Door and window trim can usually be pried off easily using a hammer and flat pry bar. Pry sideways, as shown, for the greatest leverage. To avoid damaging an adjoining piece of wood, pry forward or use a scrap of wood as a fulcrum.

If lap siding is installed with hidden nails, work from the top down. If the nails are exposed, work from the bottom up. Remove and dispose of nails as you go. If an occasional nail is difficult to remove, pound it into the wall.

Remove wood shingles as you would roofing shingles or shakes (see pages 36–37). A pitchfork or roofer's shovel makes quick work of this. Pull out most of the nails using the shovel, then use a hammer for the rest.

Vinyl siding can be removed by yanking with a pry bar, but sometimes it helps to use a zipper tool to pry the pieces apart.

Repairing sheathing

1 If a section of sheathing is rotted or otherwise damaged, cut out an area that spans from stud to stud. To find the edge of a wall stud, drill a finder hole near a sheathing nail. It may take a couple of holes to find the edge.

2 Cut out the rotted section along the inside edge of adjacent studs. This is easy work with a reciprocating saw, using the side of a stud as a guide. Remove the sheathing and any nails.

3 Where you cut alongside a stud, cut 2×4 nailers several inches longer than the opening's height. Hold each piece tight against the sheathing above and below and flush with the stud. Attach each nailer by driving 16d nails or 3-inch deck screws every 12 inches or so.

4 Cut plywood (pressure-treated, to be safe) about ¼ inch shorter and narrower than the opening. Use shims to position it with ⅛-inch gaps all around. If needed attach strips to the nailer so the patch is flush. Drive 2¼-inch deck screws about every 8 inches.

WHAT IF…
You use rigid foam insulation?

You can add a measure of extra weatherizing by replacing wood sheathing with rigid foam insulating sheathing. However be aware that this product will tightly seal a wall so it may not be recommended if you already have an interior vapor barrier or if your home is already well sealed.

Check manufacturer's instructions to be sure your framing is adequate; you may need to install bracing between the studs. After nailing the panels apply sealing tape to the joints.

STANLEY PRO TIP

Siding over existing siding

It is often possible to install new siding over old. Vinyl siding profiles may match the exposures of existing clapboard or shingles so the new siding will be well supported. The new siding will add to the thickness of the wall so you may need to add jamb extenders to your door and wall jambs so the trim can fit. Or keep the existing trim in place and butt the new siding up against it; the siding will be nearly flush with the surface of the trim.

However do this only if you are certain that the old siding is in good condition. At least a small amount of moisture will likely work its way behind the new siding, especially if it is vinyl. Install building wrap and flashings as needed to protect the old siding.

APPLYING FELT OR BUILDING PAPER

Apply roofing felt (tar paper) or building paper that is recommended for your area. Many builders use standard 15-pound roofing felt. Felt labeled "ASTM 15" meets specific standards and is the norm in many areas. It protects the sheathing against moisture infiltration yet allows some air passage so the wall can breathe.

Building paper, also called house wrap, is a strong, fibrous paper that blocks water and moisture from entering from the outside but allows moist air to pass through from the inside, preventing a buildup of moisture inside walls that can lead to mold.

Felt or building paper must be applied to walls properly to be effective. Install pieces in the correct order and make cuts carefully, so any moisture can travel downward at all points without slipping under the wrap. Install flashings (metal, self-adhesive, or both) as recommended by the window or door manufacturer or as required by local codes. Pull the wrap tight when you install it to prevent creases that could lead to slight waves in the siding.

PRESTART CHECKLIST

☐ **TIME**
Working with one or two helpers, half a day to apply 1,600 square feet or so of building wrap; more time if extensive flashings are required

☐ **TOOLS**
Hammer stapler, utility knife, hammer, chalkline, ladders and/or scaffolding

☐ **SKILLS**
Basic measuring

☐ **PREP**
Remove any old siding, nails, and building wrap from the sheathing.

☐ **MATERIALS**
Building paper or felt (tar paper), cap nails and/or staples, sealing tape, metal and self-stick flashings as needed

Roofing felt

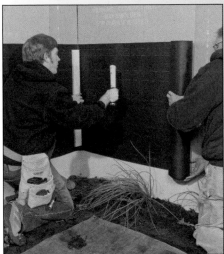

1 Working with a helper, install the bottom piece of felt so it extends 1 or 2 inches below the sill plate. Roll out a length of 8 feet or so; check that it is level and aligned with the bottom of the house. Use a hammer stapler to tack it in place. At an inside corner use a straight board to hold the felt tight to the corner as you staple.

2 Drive plenty of staples, especially if it is windy in your area. Position the successive panels so they overlap the lower panel by at least 6 inches. Use a utility knife to trim neatly around windows and doors.

Building paper

1 If you will be attaching the building paper with cap nails, use a chalkline to mark the sheathing with the locations of studs. Working with a helper, unroll the paper so it is about 2 inches below the sill plate and pull it taut. Check that it is level and aligned and drive staples or cap nails.

2 Install succeeding courses of paper so they overlap the course below by about 6 inches. If you need to make a vertical joint, overlap the pieces by 12 inches. Use recommended contractor tape to seal all the seams as well as any tears in the paper. Tape around windows and doors as well.

Sealing a rough opening

1 If you have a rough opening where a new window or door will be installed, run the paper over the opening and secure it. Make two horizontal cuts along the opening at the top and bottom. Near the center of the opening, make a vertical cut running from the top to the bottom cut.

2 At each upper corner make an 8-inch diagonal cut and temporarily fold and tape up the paper (see Step 5); this will expose some of the sheathing. Staple the side pieces so they are tautly wrapped.

3 Wrap the side pieces around the opening and up to the interior drywall (if it is installed) or onto the interior studs (if the drywall is not installed). With a hook-blade utility knife, trim away any excess building paper.

4 Cut a piece of self-stick flashing 12 inches longer than the bottom opening. Remove the bottom release sheet and apply it so it wraps up 6 inches onto the side sills. Drive two cap nails at each corner to keep the flashing in place where it has stretched.

5 If the window is installed after the siding, follow manufacturer's instructions; you may install drip-cap flashing over the top trim piece. If the window will be installed before the siding, set it into the opening and attach self-stick flashing pieces on the sides, then the top. Fold the upper flashing down; first install a drip-cap metal flashing if that is required.

APPLYING TRIM

When installing siding with uneven surfaces—such as lap siding and wood shingles—the trim boards for outside and inside corners, as well as around windows and doors, are commonly installed first. The siding is then butted up to them. For smooth-surfaced sidings like panels and board-and-batten, it is common to install the siding first, then apply the corner trims on top of the siding.

It is also possible to install lap sidings with no corner trims, precisely cutting each siding piece to form tight corners. This technique is best left to the pros; it requires extremely accurate cutting and should be attempted only by someone with excellent skills and tools. Cedar shingles can be installed with no outside corner trim (though inside corner trim is recommended) by weaving them, as shown on pages 138–139.

Unless you are using urethane or acrylic polymer moldings, be sure to protect the back sides of trim boards by priming and painting them before installing or by applying two coats of clear sealer.

PRESTART CHECKLIST

☐ **TIME**
An hour to install trims for four inside and outside corners or four simple window or door trims

☐ **TOOLS**
Hammer, drill, mitersaw, circular saw, or miter box with backsaw, tablesaw, tape measure, caulking gun, nail set, sanding block, ladders and/or scaffolding

☐ **SKILLS**
Measuring, cutting, fastening

☐ **PREP**
Install underlayment, drip-cap flashing, and valley flashing as needed (pages 40–43).

☐ **MATERIALS**
Wood, fiber-cement, or urethane trim boards; nails or screws; caulk; self-stick flashing; exterior wood putty or spackle

Outside corners

1 For the two sides of the corner trim to appear equal in width, one of them must be 1 inch narrower than the other because it is butted against a 5/4× board. (The nominal thickness is 1¼ inches; the actual thickness is 1 inch.) You can approximate equality of width by installing one 5/4×4 and one 5/4×3. But if you want to be accurate, rip-cut one of the boards 1 inch narrower than the other.

2 In most cases assembling the two pieces together before attaching them to the corner is easier and produces a neater appearance than installing one board at a time. Start with boards longer than they need to be. Drill pilot holes and drive 8d casing nails or small-headed stainless-steel screws to attach the pieces. If you have pieces that are not long enough, join them with a scarf joint (shown).

Trim board options

Choose trim boards that match the siding in texture. Cedar can be installed with either its rough or its smooth side out. Primed spruce is smooth and saves painting time. Urethane or acrylic polymer trim boards are manufactured in a variety of shapes and make it easy to produce stately moldings (see page 117).

3 For an extra measure of protection against moisture infiltration, apply 9- or 10-inch-wide self-stick flashing over the building paper or felt at the corners. Install it carefully so there will be no creases that make the wall uneven.

4 Use a mitersaw, circular saw, or miter box to cut the outside trim to length. It should extend 2 inches or so below the sill, or to whichever height you will install the siding. If the trim is not preprimed, apply primer and paint or sealer to the back and the sides. Press it firmly against the corner as you drive 10d casing nails or 3-inch small-headed screws through the sheathing and into the framing.

WHAT IF...
You install trim over the siding?

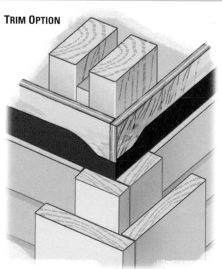

If the siding is relatively smooth—as is the case with tongue-and-groove siding—or if you don't mind V-shape gaps between the trim and the lap siding, install the siding first and then attach the outside corner trim.

Inside corner

In most cases the inside trim piece should recede visually. A 2×2 may be a bit chunky; ⁵⁄₄ stock ripped to 1 inch thick is often the best solution. Hold a couple of scrap siding pieces against the inside trim board to make sure you will have room for applying caulk after the siding is installed.

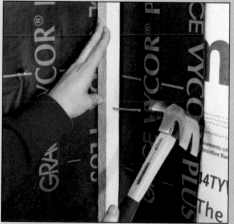

Cut the inside trim board to length, seal the backside, press the board into the corner, and attach with 10d casing nails or 3-inch screws. Drill pilot holes before nailing to avoid splits.

TRIM OPTION

If you want the trim to lie over the siding so it is more pronounced in appearance, first install small corner trim pieces as described in the previous steps and attach the siding. Then apply larger trim boards on top.

Miter-cut window trim

1 If the window has a sill and you want mitered joints for a more formal look, use a pencil and an adjustable square to scribe a reveal line about ¼ inch in from the inside of the jamb edges.

2 Measure carefully and use a miter box or a mitersaw to cut 45-degree miter cuts. The sidepieces will rest on top of the sill.

3 Seal the backs and sides of the trim boards. Drill pilot holes and drive 3d casing nails into the jamb and 8d casing nails near the outside edges. Use a nail set to drive the nailheads below the surface, fill the holes with exterior putty, and sand before applying paint.

Butt-jointed window trim

1 If the window has no sill and you want square-cut joints, cut the top (lintel) trim piece to the width of the window plus the width of the trim boards that will go on both sides. You may choose to have the lintel piece extend an inch or so past the sidepieces, but that will require you to make some fancy cuts in the siding later.

2 Install the sidepieces so they extend down past the bottom piece. Before attaching abutting pieces apply a bead of caulk to seal the joints.

WHAT IF…
You install a pretrimmed window?

Many wood windows come with trim (often brick molding) attached. If the trim does not clash with the siding, leave it in place and butt up against it. If you are installing a new window, the window may have a flange on top that should be slipped under the building wrap or you may need to install metal drip-cap flashing under the wrap and over the top trim piece.

Under eaves

You may choose to install a trim board along the underside of the eaves and perhaps along the gable end (or rake) as well. Or you may choose to install trim boards after the siding has been installed.

TYPICAL GABLE EAVE CONSTRUCTION

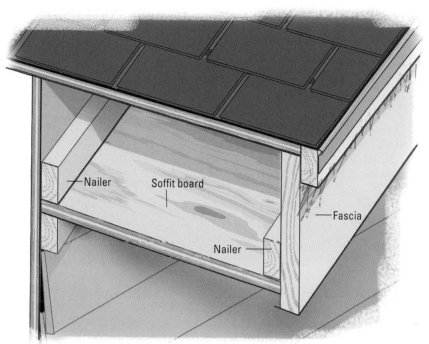

Nailer

Soffit board

Fascia

Nailer

A gable eave usually consists of a fascia board attached to blocking and a soffit board attached to the fascia and the house via hidden nailers. A trim board may be installed first and the siding butted up against it, or the trim board may be installed over the siding.

Installing molded trim boards

1 Scribe a reveal line (see Step 1, top of page 116). Install the columns by applying the recommended adhesive, then 10d galvanized casing nails.

2 Measure for the header and add twice the thickness of the header. Miter the ends and glue mitered returns in place.

3 Cut the header so it extends beyond the columns by the desired amount. Add adhesive and nail the trim in place.

4 Set the nails, fill the nail holes with exterior wood filler, and sand smooth.

INSTALLING SIDING

Most types of siding are relatively easy to install. If you own a mitersaw (see page 123), you'll find it easy to make square cuts on most types of horizontal siding. Fastening is seldom difficult; the main challenge is finding the studs to nail to (unless your house has plywood or OSB sheathing). A successful siding job mainly requires careful layout and observance of a few simple guidelines as you work.

Keeping up appearances
Lay out the job when applying horizontal siding to avoid odd slivers of material above doors and above or below windows. Siding should progress up the wall with an even exposure, and courses should line up when they meet at a corner. For layout the story pole is indispensable (see page 120). It's a tool that will help you anticipate problem areas and figure out workable solutions. Often solving one problem will introduce another, forcing a compromise. Generally you should take the solution that looks best on the most visible side of the house.

Similar principles hold true for vertical siding like board-and-batten or tongue-and-groove—thin bits of siding look bad and are difficult to cut. Panel siding should be planned so joints hit studs and to avoid narrow pieces at the ends of walls.

Allow plenty of time for laying out the job; it will save you problems later on and result in a job that looks great.

Good habits
A hallmark of an amateur siding job is horizontal siding that dips and rises with each course—a sign that someone wasn't checking for level. Similarly vertical siding must be checked for plumb. It is good to do this not only as you hold the piece in place but also after you've begun applying it. Siding can slip as you apply those first few fasteners.

Sealing the edges of unprimed siding can be awkward—it is no fun reaching for the paintbrush after every cut—but rest assured you are saving yourself headaches down the road.

And drill those pilot holes. You've invested in good material; don't mess it up with cracks and splits.

The time you spend laying out the siding installation will pay off in a great-looking, long-lasting job.

CHAPTER PREVIEW

Horizontal wood lap siding
page 120

Fiber-cement lap siding
page 126

Tongue-and-groove siding
page 128

Vinyl siding
page 130

Story pole
The story pole leaning on the window will help you lay out horizontal lap siding courses for easy installation.

Siding shingles
page 136

Shingle panels
page 142

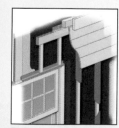

Rain-screen siding
page 143

Board-and-batten siding
page 144

Panel siding
page 146

HORIZONTAL WOOD LAP SIDING

If you choose wood lap siding, it's well worth the extra money to get preprimed siding; otherwise paint the backs and edges of the boards before installing them.

Opinions vary regarding how to fasten clapboards to a wall. Some installers maintain that it's fine to drive nails into the sheathing only, as long as it's solid plywood or OSB (oriented strand board). However driving nails into studs is a surer connection.

These steps show face-nailing (see inset illustration below), which leaves exposed nailheads. Another method is to blind-nail, driving nails near the top of the board, where they'll be covered by the next board.

Some installers don't bother with the strips of felt (Step 3), but they add extra protection from moisture infiltration and provide breathing room for condensation that can form behind the siding.

PRESTART CHECKLIST

☐ **TIME**
Working with a helper, about a day to install 600 square feet

☐ **TOOLS**
Hammer or nail gun, mitersaw or circular saw, jigsaw, tape measure, chalkline, drill, flat pry bar, level, caulking gun, utility knife, T-bevel, square, tin snips, staple gun, ladders and/or scaffolding

☐ **SKILLS**
Measuring, laying out a job, driving nails, cutting with a power saw

☐ **PREP**
Cover the sheathing with building wrap and install trim boards and flashings as needed.

☐ **MATERIALS**
Wood lap siding, board for story pole, felt strips, staples, board and flashing for water table, stainless steel or galvanized siding nails, caulk, primer or sealer

1 To determine an attractive reveal (the amount of the board face that is exposed), hold or tack a few pieces of siding on the wall near a trim board to see how it looks. This is 8-inch-wide beveled siding with a 5½-inch reveal.

2 Make a story pole to help you lay out the siding courses. Mark along 1×2 or 1×4 with evenly spaced lines to represent the exposure you have chosen. To ensure that you don't hold the story pole upside down, mark an arrow pointing to the bottom.

HORIZONTAL SIDING LAYOUT

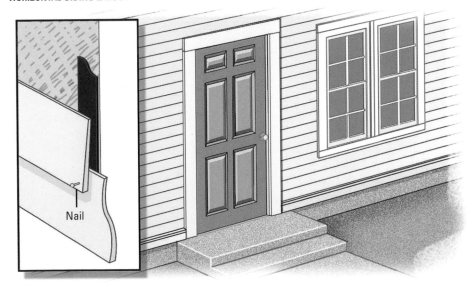

Nail

Plan the siding courses so as to minimize narrow slivers above or below windows and doors. You will likely need to make compromises. In the layout shown there is a full piece of siding over the doorway and half-width pieces above and below the window.

If all the windows are at the same height, you may choose to make them the focal points, at the expense of a narrow piece over the door. When siding the whole house, keep in mind that you will need to maintain the layout all the way around.

3 Determine the locations of studs. Staple a 2-inch-wide strip of felt over each stud, using a level to help position them plumb before fastening.

4 Snap chalklines indicating the exact stud centers. Prepare for installing a 1×6 or 1×8 water table along the bottom of the installation (typically 1 or 2 inches below the sill plate) by snapping chalklines to help you keep the boards straight.

5 Attach the water table by driving two or three nails at each stud. If the boards are not long enough to span the length of a wall, join them using a scarf joint or a simple butt joint. Apply caulk to the edge of one board and press the next board into the caulk.

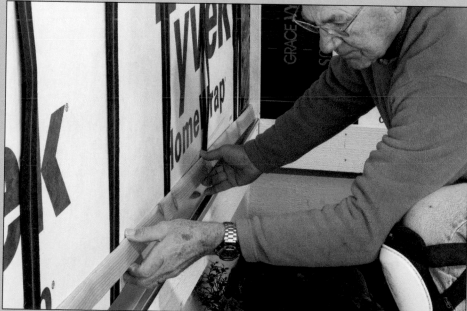

6 Use tin snips to cut pieces of drip cap or Z-flashing and install them against the wall and over the top edge of the water table. Overlap any joints by at least 3 inches. Rip-cut 1¼-inch-wide pieces of siding to be placed on top of the water table. This piece will cause the bottom siding piece to slightly flare out from the wall at its bottom. Cut the ripped pieces to fit and nail them ¼ inch above the flashing.

WHAT IF...
You have wood sheathing?

Some installers place short strips of felt or metal flashing at the butt joints only. This is the right method to use if you are driving nails into the sheathing only—in which case the butt joints will occur at random locations.

7 To plan the layout for the courses, hold the story pole on top of the water table and next to a window or door. If the layout will cause narrow slivers above or below the window, raise or lower the pole as needed. Test the layout at other windows as well.

8 At each corner use the story pole to mark the wall with layout lines. You may choose to mark every course or every third or fourth course. Mark the trim pieces rather than the wall; marks placed on the wall will be hidden by the pieces below.

WHAT IF...
You compensate with varied exposures?

In some cases you can install some of the courses with slightly narrower exposures so they will come out even at the bottom or top of a window. To lay this out use the story pole as a "swing stick." Tilt it until one of its lines is at the desired height; this will evenly compress the exposure of each course. Holding the story pole in this position, use the lines to mark the wall for the intervening courses.

12 Measure from a corner to the center of a stud. Cut boards of succeeding courses so their joints are staggered by at least 16 inches. One efficient method of installation is to have one person cutting while two people measure and install siding pieces. This is especially helpful once you get up on a ladder or scaffolding.

9 If you are installing all around a house, the courses must meet (or at least come within 1 inch of meeting) at all the corners. A water level (shown), transit, or laser level can help you make marks that are level with each other all the way around.

10 Check the board ends for square. Typically about one in ten will be miscut at the lumber mill. Use a mitersaw or a circular saw and a layout square guide to cut the pieces square.

11 Apply a generous coat of primer or sealer to the board ends. This is especially important for ends you have cut, but even factory-cut ends will benefit from extra protection. If the siding is not prestained, it is a good idea to apply paint or sealer to the backs of the boards as well.

13 You'll be doing plenty of cutting, so anchor a mitersaw on a stable platform and provide supports on either side for the boards to rest on. Or build a table for cutting with a circular saw.

14 Before you install a board against a trim piece, apply a modest bead of exterior caulk to the side of the trim.

STANLEY PRO TIP

Staying straight

Long siding boards are flexible and some are a bit crowned or twisted. To make sure they stay straight, you may choose to snap chalklines on the wall located at the tops of the siding pieces (rather than at the bottoms, where the layout lines are). You usually need to do this only every third or fourth board if you check the other boards every few feet with a spacing tool. Alternatively have one person sight along the board while the other one nails.

15 Press the board into the caulk, check to be sure that the other end is aligned with a stud center or fits snugly against a trim piece, and drive nails into studs. Wherever you will drive a nail less than 1 inch from a board end, drill a pilot hole first, to avoid splitting the board.

16 For succeeding courses drive nails about 1½ inches above the bottom of the board so that they drive through the underlying board near its top. (Some installers prefer to drive the nails higher so they miss the underlying board, but that can lead to cracks.) At a butt joint apply caulk to the end of one board and push the boards together. Drill angled pilot holes before driving nails.

17 Snap lines indicating the bottom of the boards. Every 6 to 8 feet, tack nails onto which you can set the board before nailing. You may find it handy to make a spacing tool like the one shown on pages 59 and 61 to avoid measuring each time.

WHAT IF...
You choose a scarf joint?

Some installers prefer to use scarf joints where two boards meet. If done well scarf joints are less visible than simple butt joints. However it can be difficult to make hundreds of accurate scarf joints, and well-caulked butt joints are usually not noticeable.

20 To make a cutout for a receptacle or other obstruction, drill a hole or two inside the cutout lines and cut with a jigsaw.

21 At the top of a window or door, you may need to install a sliver that is the same thickness as the siding on each side, so the piece installed over the window will be correctly flared out.

18 To mark for notch-cutting around a window, hold the board in place and mark the sides. To find the depth of the notch, measure from the bottom of the next-lowest piece to the bottom of the piece to be cut and mark for a cut that will produce the correct exposure.

19 Notch cuts usually need to be precise because they will not be covered with trim. First make the two short cuts at either end of the notch. Make a plunge cut for the long cut. To make a plunge cut, retract the circular saw's guard, tilt the saw up, turn on the motor, and slowly lower the blade. Finish cutting the corners using a handsaw or jigsaw.

22 Use a T-bevel to capture an angle along a gable end. Tighten the T-bevel's nut and transfer the angle to the board to be cut. Once you have cut one or two pieces that fit snugly, you may use cutoff scraps as templates for the next cuts.

23 At the roofline install the angle-cut pieces 2 inches above the flashing, to ensure that they won't get soaked. Apply plenty of primer or sealer to the cut ends before installing the boards.

24 Apply caulk to the joints between siding and trim. Prime and paint the boards or apply stain and/or clear sealer.

FIBER-CEMENT LAP SIDING

This product comes in 12-foot lengths. These steps show 8¼-inch-wide boards installed with 7-inch exposures; you can choose narrower or wider boards and exposures. Layout and installation is generally the same as for wood lap siding (pages 120–125). Here are the differences:
■ At the bottom of the wall, there is a starter strip rather than a water table board.
■ Because the material is very rigid, you can blind-nail the boards near the top, where the nailheads will be covered by the next course.
■ Because fiber-cement expands with rises in humidity, the boards should be cut ¼ inch short so there is a ⅛-inch gap at each joint.
   Like wood siding the ends should be coated with primer before you install them. Cutting calls for different techniques and tools but is not difficult.

PRESTART CHECKLIST

☐ **TIME**
   Working with a helper, about a day to install 600 square feet

☐ **TOOLS**
   Hammer or nail gun; mitersaw; hand shears, grinder, or circular saw; speed square; tape measure; chalkline; drill; flat pry bar; level; caulking gun; utility knife; T-bevel; tin snips; staple gun; ladders and/or scaffolding

☐ **SKILLS**
   Measuring, laying out a job, cutting, driving nails

☐ **PREP**
   Cover the sheathing with building wrap and install trim boards and flashings as needed.

☐ **MATERIALS**
   Fiber-cement siding, starter strip for the bottom, board to make story pole, strips of metal flashing or felt, staples, stainless-steel or galvanized siding nails, primer and paint

1 Apply building paper, self-stick flashings at corners and around windows, and metal flashings as needed (see pages 112–117). Snap vertical chalklines indicating the centers of studs. Use a story pole to lay out the courses. Because there is no water table, you can probably raise or lower the bottom piece a couple of inches to achieve the course layout you desire. Make sure the bottom course will be at least 6 inches above grade and at least 2 inches above a driveway or sidewalk.

STANLEY PRO TIP: **Cutting fiber-cement siding**

For most cutting a power hand shear (above) is recommended because it cuts without creating dust. Inexpensive shears are often difficult to use, so you may want to rent a professional-quality model. Shears make only straight cuts or slight curves, so you may need another tool to cut notches.
   You can also cut using a circular saw equipped with a masonry-cutting blade (above center), but wear a dust mask so you don't breathe in the resulting clouds of dust.
   A grinder (above) is useful for small cutouts but, like the circular saw, generates plenty of dust.

2 To get the bottom board to flare out slightly, install a ripped piece of siding (shown) or a metal starter strip.

3 Lay out for the courses by marking the trim or snap chalklines indicating the tops of the boards (lines indicating the bottoms will be covered by the underlying pieces). To speed up installation tack nails at these lines and butt the boards up to the nails when installing.

4 Cut boards ¼ inch short so that there will be a ⅛-inch gap at each end. Apply a generous coat of primer to all cut edges prior to installation. Apply a bead of caulk on the trim or abutting board before installing. Drive nails about 1½ inches from the top of the boards where they will be hidden by the next course.

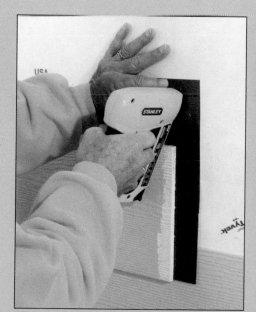

5 At butt joints slip a strip of felt or a short piece of 3-inch-wide metal flashing behind the boards, as shown. Alternatively apply strips of felt over all the studs, as shown on page 121.

6 Fiber-cement is prone to cracking so drill pilot holes first wherever you will drive a nail less than 2 inches from the end.

STANLEY PRO TIP

Finishing and maintaining fiber-cement siding

Fiber-cement siding is a hardy, long-lasting material; its only weak points are unsealed edges or abrasions.

To protect the material caulk all the joints and smooth the caulk with your finger or a damp rag so it blends in with the boards' texture. Apply primer and two coats of high-quality exterior paint.

To repair a dent apply epoxy wood filler as shown on page 158. Scrape smooth, then scratch with a screwdriver or putty knife to more or less imitate the faux wood grain. Prime the patch and paint.

TONGUE-AND-GROOVE SIDING

A variety of siding types fit together by means of tongues and grooves or over- and underlapping edges. Because the overlap is less than on other types of siding, these provide somewhat less protection from the elements. Check to make sure the siding you choose has a successful track record in your region.

Depending on how the pieces fit together, some jointed sidings can be fully attached by blind-nailing through a tongue or underlap that will be covered by the course above. Other types require face-nailing as well. The area where you will blind-drive the fasteners is thin, so there is a danger of cracking the wood when you drive a nail. Preempt any splits by drilling pilot holes. The extra step is worth the effort: A cracked board is seriously compromised and may allow water to seep behind. Some installers choose to drive small-headed stainless-steel screws instead of nails. Or you could use a power stapler, which is less likely than a nailer to split boards.

PRESTART CHECKLIST

☐ **TIME**
With a helper, a day for 600 square feet

☐ **TOOLS**
Power nailer or stapler, hammer, drill, mitersaw or circular saw, tablesaw, tape measure, story pole, chalkline, drill, flat pry bar, level, caulking gun, utility knife, T-bevel, tin snips, staple gun, ladders and/or scaffolding

☐ **SKILLS**
Cutting with a circular saw, measuring

☐ **PREP**
Cover the sheathing with building wrap. Install trim boards and flashings as needed.

☐ **MATERIALS**
Wood tongue-and-groove or shiplap siding, strips of felt, staples, stainless-steel or galvanized siding nails or screws, exterior stain/sealer

1 Apply building wrap and prepare the walls as shown on pages 112–117. If you live in a damp climate, consider using the rain-screen method (page 143). Apply self-stick flashing to corners and around windows and doors and apply flashings as needed. You may choose to install strips of felt at the studs as shown on page 121 or use the technique shown here in Step 5. Snap chalklines indicating the centers of all the studs. Use a story pole (page 120) to lay out the courses and mark the layout all around the house if needed (pages 122–123). You may choose to rip-cut the bottom piece in order to achieve the desired layout.

JOINTED SIDING PROFILES

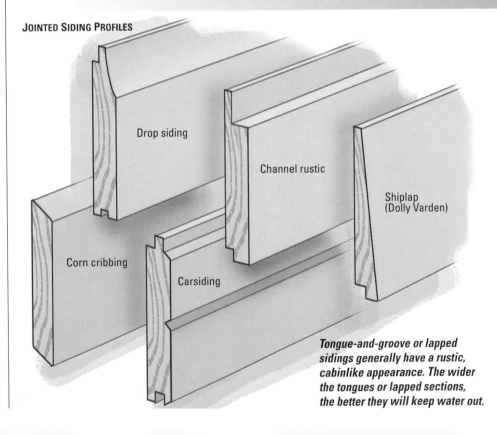

Drop siding

Channel rustic

Shiplap
(Dolly Varden)

Corn cribbing

Carsiding

Tongue-and-groove or lapped sidings generally have a rustic, cabinlike appearance. The wider the tongues or lapped sections, the better they will keep water out.

2 Take special care to protect the backs, edges, and cut ends. Apply generous coats of sealer, using a roller or a sprayer. Or build a long trough lined with plastic sheeting and soak each board in sealer for several seconds.

3 Out of a scrap piece of 1× lumber or siding, cut a "preacher" to aid in marking the boards for cutting. The preacher should be about 8 inches longer than the width of the siding boards. Cut notches so the preacher will fit fairly tightly around the board to be marked.

4 Cut the boards to fit snugly against trim pieces or abutting siding pieces. If you have a mitersaw or radial-arm saw, attach it firmly to a table and provide supports for the siding boards on either side. Or set up a comfortable cutting station for using a circular saw (shown).

5 Apply strips of self-stick flashing (or WSU) to the area behind each butt joint, as shown. Flexible flashing is a good choice when applying shiplap because it can mold around the lap and still effectively seal out moisture.

6 Apply a stain/sealer recommended for use in your area. Use a paintbrush to work sealer into all the joints, especially the undersides of boards. Apply several coats of sealer and inspect to make sure all joints are well protected. Apply high-quality exterior caulk to all joints.

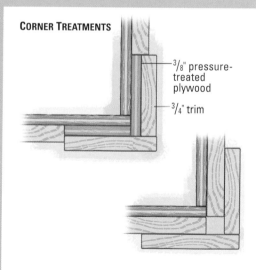

CORNER TREATMENTS

3/8" pressure-treated plywood

3/4" trim

You may choose to install corner trim first and butt the siding up to it as shown on pages 114–115. If you want the trim to be more pronounced, install the siding first and then apply the trim over the siding. For a less pronounced reveal, attach strips of 3/8-inch pressure-treated plywood to the insides of the corner trims and install the corners before you install the siding (top).

VINYL SIDING

Vinyl siding cuts easily, goes up quickly, produces uniform reveals almost automatically, and needs minimal caulking and no painting. But don't take the job lightly: The walls must be well prepared and the pieces installed correctly to prevent leaks and siding failure.

With vinyl siding some moisture will seep behind the siding and must be allowed to escape at the bottom around weep holes, much like those in a brick wall (page 104). Seepage won't be a problem if you correctly install building wrap and flashings or if the underlying siding is in sound condition.

The higher the vinyl gauge—that is, the thicker it is—the better it will perform. Vinyl that is 0.048 inch thick is significantly stronger than 0.040-inch-thick vinyl. Vinyl siding does not need to be painted.

The basic rule is "hang loose." Because vinyl expands and contracts with changes in the weather, nails should not be driven fully tight, and pieces should be cut so there are ¼-inch gaps between panels and trims.

PRESTART CHECKLIST

☐ **TIME**
With a helper, 600 square feet per day

☐ **TOOLS**
Hammer, mitersaw or circular saw, tape measure, clamps, chalkline, drill, pry bar, square, level, story pole, caulking gun, utility knife, T-bevel, tin snips, staple gun, snap-lock punch tool

☐ **SKILLS**
Measuring, laying out a job, cutting

☐ **PREP**
Apply building wrap, trim, and flashings.

☐ **MATERIALS**
Siding, trim to match (inside and outside corner posts, J-channel, starter strip, window and door starters), flashing, stainless-steel or galvanized nails, caulk

1 Apply building wrap and prepare the walls as shown on pages 112–117. Apply self-stick flashing to corners and around windows and doors and apply flashings as needed. If you live in a damp climate, consider using the rain-screen method (page 143). You may choose to install strips of felt at the studs as shown on page 121. Snap chalklines indicating the centers of all the studs. Use a story pole to determine where to start at the bottom; adjust the layout up or down as needed to avoid narrow slivers above or below windows and doors. (There is no need to mark for the courses; they are automatically determined when you snap the siding pieces together.) Mark the bottom of the layout all around the house if needed (pages 122–123).

The total ensemble

Show a detailed drawing of your home's exterior to your supplier, who should help you make a list of all the parts you will need. There are trim posts for outside corners and inside corners. Around windows and doors you may choose to keep existing wood trim and install narrow J-channel or install wide vinyl trim. A starter strip is needed at the bottom of the wall. You may also buy vinyl fascia boards.

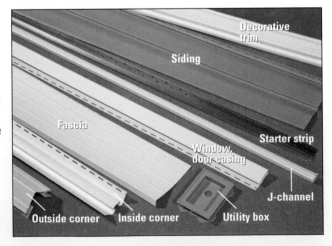

Decorative trim

Siding

Fascia

Window, door casing

Starter strip

J-channel

Outside corner

Inside corner

Utility box

2 Chalk a level line indicating the top of the starter strip. Align a strip about 3 inches short of the corners and drive nails into the centers of the slots. Drive the nails loosely (see Step 14, page 133). Where two strips abut leave a ¼-inch gap.

3 Cut an outside corner post to run from ½ inch below the bottom of the starter strip to the eave or gable underhang. Hold the post ¼ inch below the underhang (so it will be ¾ inch below the starter strip) and loosely drive a nail at the top of the top slot. Slip the post flanges behind the starter strip flanges. Drive the other nails loosely (see Step 14, page 133) into the centers of slots.

4 If the corner is not long enough, cut the lower piece 1½ inches longer than the distance to the bottom of the starter strip and make a splice: Cut 1 inch from the flanges of the lower piece and slide the lower piece under the upper piece by ¾ inch. (This will leave a ¼ inch gap in the flanges, and the post will hang ¾ inch below the starter strip.)

STANLEY PRO TIP: **Cutting vinyl siding and trim**

Vinyl siding can be cut with a sharp utility knife, but there are easier ways. Install a circular saw blade backwards so the teeth are reversed, and cut using a large layout square as a guide

(above). Or cut with a mitersaw or radial-arm saw with a reversed blade.

To cut flanges and make small notches, simply use tin snips (above right). If you need

to add a nailing slot to a siding piece that has had the nailing flange removed, drill two ³⁄₁₆-inch holes about an inch apart and cut out the material between them.

Cut flange and back (all but face) even with window trim

5 Install inside corner posts in a similar way, with a ¼-inch gap at the top and hanging ¾ inch below the starter strip.

6 Install J-channels around a window with trim. (If the window has no trim, you may want to install wider casing.) Cut each sidepiece to the height of the window plus the width of the top and bottom channels. Cut the flange and back even with the trim.

7 At the bottom end of each sidepiece, make a miter cut in the face of the channel. Nail the channels in place.

WHAT IF... You choose decorative trim?

Most vinyl siding manufacturers offer a variety of decorative trims for windows and doors. Some include a corner block, which is installed after the top and sidepieces. A "crown" assembly attaches over the sidepieces and includes a return piece. All of these parts come with specific installation instructions to ensure that water will flow down and away from the house.

11 Install J-channels along the underside of a gable. Miter-cut only one of the faces and then slip it over the face of the other piece.

12 To flash along a roof, snap a chalkline and install J-channel 1 inch above the shingles.

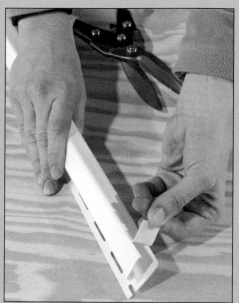

8 Cut the top piece to the width of the window plus the side channels. Snip and bend the tabs to fit down into the sidepieces (next step) and miter-cut the faces at the corner.

9 Install the top trim piece by slipping the bent tabs down into the side channels to provide a downward path for moisture. At each end the miter-cut face of the top piece fits over the face of the sidepiece.

10 Cut the bottom piece as shown so the sidepiece's tab can slip down into it. Install the bottom piece so its face is under the miter-cut face of the sidepiece.

13 Once all the trim pieces are in place, the siding panels can go up. Cut the panels to fit loosely, with ¼-inch gaps at the trim pieces. Slip a panel into position, then push up firmly at the bottom until it snaps onto the lower piece's flange (or the starter strip). Keep pressing and slide your hand along the bottom to ensure that the joint is secure all along its length.

14 Always take care to have a ¹⁄₃₂- to ⅛-inch gap (about the thickness of a dime) between the nailhead and the vinyl. You should be able to slide the strip side to side a bit.

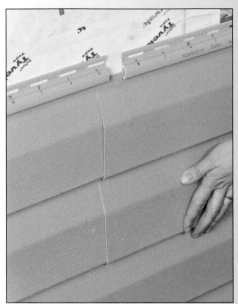

15 At a seam overlap the panels by 1 inch. Cut back the flange of one piece if necessary to maintain at least a ¼-inch gap between flanges.

16 Shut off the water and remove a spigot. Use a drill with a hole saw or a utility knife to cut a hole that is ¼ inch away from the pipe at all points. Caulk around the pipe and reinstall the spigot.

17 Where you cannot remove an obstacle, use wraparound boxes. Install the box, cut a hole in the siding and attach it, and snap on the trim. Or make a seam joint at the obstruction and cut notches in the ends of each piece.

21 Slip the siding into the flange until the indentations along the notch are captured.

22 Use a straight board or a siding panel to mark for cutting an angle along a roofline. You may have to cut a rough angle first for the panel to set close enough to the roof to mark the angle. Make the angle cut.

23 Check the angle cut before cutting the panel to length. When you are satisfied with the cuts, snap the panel into the flange and slide it into the J-channel.

18 Trim light fixtures and receptacles using snap-on utility boxes or custom-cut pieces of J-channel or other trim to fit.

19 When marking for cutting around a window, allow a ¼-inch gap between the panel and the J-channel or other trim. Holding the panel in place, mark the two sides, then measure for the depth of the cutout by determining how far the panel needs to come up so it can snap into place.

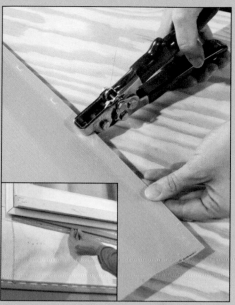

20 Cut the notch and use a snap-lock punch tool to make a series of indentations. The indented flange can now snap into a channel, eliminating the need for nails. Install the flange (inset).

24 To capture the angle for a gable, hold a board against a scrap piece as shown and scribe the angle. Measure for the length of the bottom edge of the panel and subtract ½ inch. You may need a helper to bend the panel into place.

25 At the very top of a gable, you may need to drive one nail. Cover the nail with exterior caulk and paint the caulk to match the siding.

26 Apply caulk only to the joints between channels and wood trim; do not seal the joints between the panels and vinyl trim.

SIDING SHINGLES

Cedar shingles take more time to install than most other types of siding, but they create a richly textured look. Shingles can be installed only if the sheathing is boards, plywood, or OSB.

Shingles should be installed to provide triple coverage, with three layers of shingles covering the wall. To achieve this the exposures should be slightly less than one-third the length of the shingle. For example, in these pages 16-inch-long shingles are installed with 5-inch exposures.

You could first install outside corner trim made of 1× boards and then butt the shingles up to the trim, but a woven corner (pages 138–139) is more attractive. A woven inside corner is much more difficult to achieve, so the usual practice is to install inside corner trim prior to shingling.

Because shingles can swell slightly, it is sometimes recommended that you provide ⅛-inch gaps between the shingles. However as long as the shingles are not completely dried out, they will shrink slightly after installation, so gapping is usually not needed. Check with your supplier to be sure.

PRESTART CHECKLIST

☐ **TIME**
With a helper, a day for 400 square feet

☐ **TOOLS**
Staple gun or hammer, circular saw, tape measure, block plane, chalkline, drill, flat pry bar, level, story pole, caulking gun, utility knife, T-bevel, tin snips, ladders and/or scaffolding

☐ **SKILLS**
Basic carpentry skills

☐ **PREP**
Cover sheathing with building wrap; install trim boards and flashings.

☐ **MATERIALS**
Wood shingles, cedar wood trim, stainless-steel or galvanized nails or staples, caulk, primer and paint or sealer

1 Apply building wrap and prepare the walls as shown on pages 112–117. Apply self-stick flashing to corners and around windows and doors and apply flashings as needed. Take special care not to crease the wrap or the flashings.

2 Apply trim around the windows and doors as needed. If you will weave the shingles at outside corners (see Steps 6–7 on page 138), no outside corner trim is needed.

DECORATIVE SHINGLES

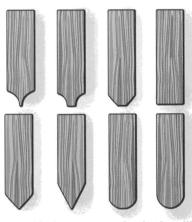

Fancy-cut shingles are expensive, but installing only a couple of rows or a small section of them can really spice things up. You can also cut your own decorative shingles out of standard shingles; just be sure they are of uniform width. Install decoratives over a course of standard shingles or drop them down a bit, to ensure that the wall is double-covered with shingles at all points.

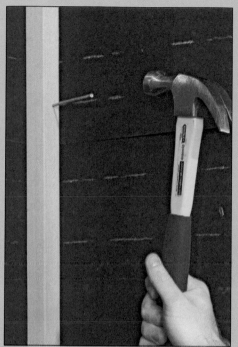

3 Use a story pole to lay out courses and to avoid narrow pieces above or below windows and doors. You may choose to raise or lower the bottom course to achieve the desired layout (see step 10 on page 139) or use the swing-stick method (page 122). Mark the layout all around the house.

4 Install inside corner trim pieces. These should not be too visible but must be wide enough to provide room for caulking after the shingles are installed. A 1×1 board ripped from ⁵⁄₄ cedar decking is often the ideal size. Hold up several layers of shingles to make sure the trim is thick enough.

5 Install the first starter-course piece at a corner. It should run past the corner by about 1 inch. Use a small level to hold it plumb and attach with two nails or staples. Less-expensive lower-grade shingles can be used as the starter course.

PRO TIP: **A pneumatic nailer or stapler speeds the job**

You can hand-nail shingles, but the job goes faster with a pneumatic nailer or stapler. A stapler is used most often because it is less likely to split the shingles. Even if you are shingling just a single wall, renting power equipment will be worth the cost.

Adjust the stapler so it drives the staples just flush and does not indent them. When you hit a stud, the staple may not sink in completely; drive the staple flush with a hammer.

Use galvanized nails or staples for most of the job. Stainless-steel nails are the best choice wherever the heads will show.

WHAT IF...
You trim outside corners?

You may choose to install corner trim pieces (see pages 114–115) and simply butt the shingles up to the trim boards.

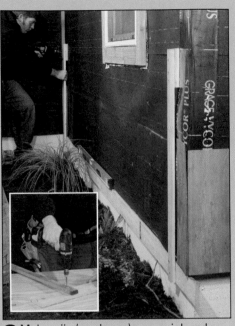

6 Install a piece on the other side of the corner butted against the first piece. Use a utility knife to roughly cut the first piece.

7 Use a small plane or Surform tool to trim the shingle edge flush. When building a corner trim and plane each piece before moving on to the next course.

8 Make a jig (as shown) as a quick and failsafe way to keep the courses even. Use a straight 1×4 as the guide and 1×2s as the hangers. Check it for level and then fasten it with 3-inch screws.

STANLEY PRO TIP: **Cutting shingles**

You can cut shingles using a tablesaw, a chop saw, or a radial-arm saw. In the example shown the miter gauge is used to cut corner pieces at a slight angle, which eliminates the need to

knife-trim (perhaps even planing smooth) the corner pieces. If you use a circular saw, clamp the shingle first to keep your fingers away from the blade. If the grain is straight and knot-free,

use a utility knife to make simple cuts. Slice once or twice, then snap the shingle apart. You may need to touch up the split with a block plane (Step 7).

9 The starter course is made of two layers of shingles. Attach the second layer so its joints are offset at least 1½ inches from the joints of the underlying layer. You will likely need to cut the last pieces in each row.

10 Build up the corners. The bottom course (which is on top of the starter course) may be anywhere from 1 to 4 inches above the starter course, depending on your layout. To maintain correct exposures use a homemade exposure guide. Drive nails or staples about 1 inch above the exposure so that they will be covered. Also check your layout marks every few courses. Trim and plane a corner board before you install the next course.

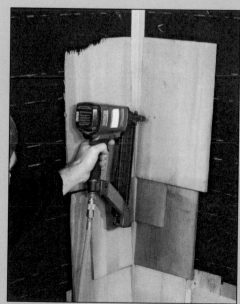

11 Build the inside corners in the same way; you will not need to plane any shingle edges.

12 Once you have built up the corners by about 10 courses, snap a chalkline to mark the bottom of the next course. Attach vertical pieces to a long, straight guide and attach to the wall as shown. Place shingles on the guide board and fasten them, offsetting joints by at least 1½ inches.

13 At window and door corners, install wide notch-cut shingles. Avoid having a joint closer than 1 inch from the corner.

14 Above a window or door, you will need to cut and install strips of the correct thickness so that the full-thickness pieces installed over them will be correctly flared out from the wall.

15 Turn off the water and remove a hose spigot. Use a drill and a hole saw to cut a neat hole in the shingle. The hole should be large enough that there is at least a ¼-inch gap between the pipe and the shingle to avoid damage from condensation. Caulk the gap before replacing the spigot.

WHAT IF...
You are installing fiber-cement shingle panels?

You can quickly achieve the look of painted shingles by installing fiber-cement panels made to look like shingles. Some panels have the appearance of shingles that are staggered in exposure length.

The panels are designed to provide triple-coverage as with wood shingles. You cannot weave the corners, so first install outside corner trim. Cut the panels and install them using many of the techniques for lap siding shown on pages 126–127. Install a starter strip at the bottom. Drive all nails into studs.

16 Set a scrap of wood on the roof and use a T-bevel to capture the angle for cutting along a gable. Where possible install the angled pieces first, then fill in with full-length pieces.

17 Along a roof install flashing, then install shingles 1 or 2 inches above the flashing. To cut a series of shingles that follow a roofline, align four or five of them on a worktable and snap a chalkline across them all, using the T-bevel as a guide.

18 Once all the shingles are installed, apply caulk at all the trim joints. Apply two or more coats of sealer or two coats of primer before painting.

WHAT IF…
You are installing individual fiber-cement shingles?

Individual fiber-cement shingles are also available. They install in virtually the same way as standard shingles. You will first install outside corner boards as well as a starter strip at the bottom of the wall. Drive nails into sheathing, which must be solid plywood or OSB.

SHINGLE PANELS

Cedar shingle panels consist of shingles attached to a plywood or OSB backerboard. The backerboard is sealed to repel moisture. Each panel is a single course. The panels stack on top of each other to automatically create the exposure and have interlocking end joints as well. The panels are available in a variety of exposures. Panels can be installed with outside corner trim boards, shingled corner boards that match the panels, or one-piece shaped corners, shown in these steps.

Prepare the walls as you would for standard cedar shingles by applying building wrap, applying self-stick flashings at the corners and around windows and doors, and installing metal flashings. You may also choose to install felt strips covering the studs or short strips at each butt joint (page 121). Snap chalklines at the centers of studs. Install trim pieces at the inside corners and install any needed trim boards (at least 1 inch thick) around windows and doors.

The panels should be attached with nails or screws driven into studs so that they can be installed over nonsolid sheathing.

1 Install outside corners. Use a story pole (see page 120) to determine the desired height at which to install the panels so you won't end up with narrow slivers at the tops or bottoms of windows and doors (see page 122). To achieve the desired layout, you may need to rip-cut the bottom panel.

2 Install a furring strip at the bottom of the wall to flare the bottom course out from the wall. Press the bottom panel against the corner and attach it by driving blind nails into studs. Also face-drive nails into the bottom sill.

3 Cut panels with a circular saw and a square. Cut from the back to minimize splintering. The shingle widths are random so most joints will be automatically offset, although it does not matter if the joints coincide on adjoining courses. Attach subsequent courses with blind nails near the top of the panels.

4 Cut panels to fit around windows and other obstructions. You will likely need to rip-cut panels at the top of the wall and angle-cut panels at a gable end. Caulk the joints and apply sealer.

RAIN-SCREEN SIDING

In some areas of the country and especially on some newer homes, siding sometimes buckles, twists, or rots. The problem is often attributed to moisture attacking the back of the siding. (A certain amount of moisture is expected, but it should have a way to dry out.) Why this happens is the subject of much study. Possible reasons include:

- Lesser-quality siding that has not been back-primed or sealed
- Rigid foam insulation and older, less-permeable types of house wrap, which prevent moisture from dissipating
- Inadequate caulking, which allows too much water to infiltrate behind the siding
- Poor flashing, which also provides an inward pathway for moisture
- A vapor barrier (usually a plastic sheet or foil facing on insulation batts) that has been incorrectly installed between the studs and the sheathing (it should be between the studs and the drywall or not installed at all). This traps moisture where it can damage sheathing and the back of siding.

In most areas and for most homes, the solution is to follow the instructions presented in this book: Properly wrap the sheathing; install self-adhesive flashings at corners, windows, and doors; and provide extra protection at the butt joints of the siding. If you install vinyl siding, take care to provide pathways for moisture to travel down and exit at the bottom of the wall.

For an extra measure of insurance against rot, some professionals install rain-screen protection, which allows air to enter the space behind the siding. It also allows moisture to travel down the wall behind the siding and exit out the bottom. The idea is simple, but the installation can be complex.

The siding (and the water table, if any) is held away from the wall by means of vertical furring strips, which are installed over the building wrap and are themselves covered with felt or self-stick flashing. At the bottom special venting material is installed to allow air in but keep bugs out. At the top moldings are installed in special ways so they allow air to pass through. If you have reason to believe that excessive moisture may be a problem for your home, consult with a professional siding installer to see whether a rain-screen installation is the solution.

RAIN-SCREEN ANATOMY

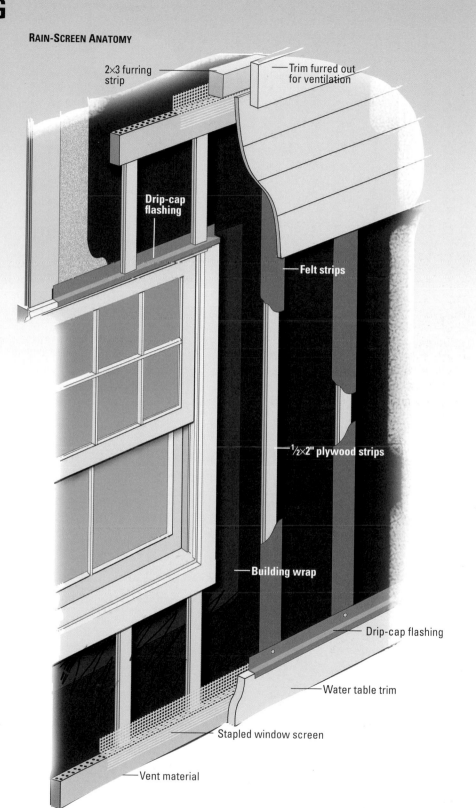

BOARD-AND-BATTEN SIDING

True board-and-batten, as shown on these two pages, is made with vertically installed wide boards and narrow battens fastened over the gaps between the boards. To install siding panels and battens to mimic the appearance of board-and-batten, see page 150. In appearance board-and-batten siding can look rustic or modern, depending on how rough the lumber is and its finish.

Perhaps the most common arrangement uses 1×10 boards and 1×2 or 1×3 batten. You can also use 1×8 or 1×12 boards and 1×4 battens. To seal out moisture the boards should be in sound condition and free of open knots, and the battens should lap at least ¾ inch onto the boards on both sides. Cedar is a good lumber choice because it is soft; harder wood, like pressure-treated pine, will not seal as well and is more likely to crack.

Board-and-batten can be installed onto solid plywood or OSB sheathing. If your sheathing is not solid, you will need to first attach horizontal furring strips (see box, below right).

1 Prepare the walls as you would for other wood sidings by applying building wrap, self-stick flashings at the corners and around windows and doors, and metal flashings as required (see pages 112–117).

2 All around the house install a 1×6 or wider water table, with its bottom edge 2 inches below the sill plate. Snap level chalklines to help you keep the water-table boards straight and attach them by driving two or three nails at each stud. If the boards are not long enough to span across a wall, join them with a scarf joint (page 124) or a simple butt joint. Attach drip cap or Z-flashing over the water table.

PRESTART CHECKLIST

☐ **TIME**
   With a helper, a day for 800 square feet

☐ **TOOLS**
   Hammer or nail gun, mitersaw or circular saw, jigsaw, tape measure, chalkline, drill, pry bar, level, caulking gun, utility knife, T-bevel, tin snips, stapler

☐ **SKILLS**
   Measuring, laying out a job, driving nails, cutting with a power saw

☐ **PREP**
   Cover the sheathing with building wrap and install trim boards and flashings.

☐ **MATERIALS**
   Boards and battens, board for the water table, Z-flashing, stainless-steel or galvanized siding nails, caulk, primer

WHAT IF...
You don't have solid plywood or OSB sheathing?

In some areas it is common to attach vertical 1×2 furring strips before installing board-and-batten siding. If your sheathing is not solid plywood or OSB, these strips are needed to provide a nailing surface. Attach strips around windows and doors, then lay out and attach horizontal strips every 16 inches. Nail the strips to framing members.

Furring strips bring the siding out from the sheathing ¾ inch. As a result you may need to rip-cut and attach wood extenders onto your window and door jambs so there will not be a gap between the trim and the jambs.

3 On each wall measure from the corners to plan a layout that avoids narrow slivers next to doors and windows. Take into account both the width of the boards and the thickness of the gap between boards. For instance if you are installing 1×10 boards that are 9⅜ inches wide (measure to be sure because they can vary in width) with a ⅝-inch gap, figure 10 inches for each board.

4 You may rip-cut the first board to achieve the desired layout. Cut the length to fit or to a determined height if you will stack boards on top (Step 7). Place the board on the water table about ¼ inch shy of the corner, use a level to check that it is plumb, and drive pairs of nails every 16 inches. Place the nails about 2 inches from the sides of the board. The nails should be long enough to poke through the sheathing.

5 Attach the next boards in the same way. Use spacers (⅝-inch plywood is shown here) to maintain fairly consistent gaps. Every third or fourth board, check for plumb and make adjustments as needed. (The battens will cover modest imperfections.) When you meet a window or door siding, cut the board so that it is about ¼ inch above the trim's drip-cap flashing.

6 Use a T-bevel (see page 125) to capture the angle at a rake end. Wherever possible cut the angle first, then hold the piece in place and mark the other side for cutting to length.

7 Where boards are not long enough to reach all the way up to an eave or rake, install all the boards at the same height. Cut and install Z-flashing over the boards and install the upper pieces ¼ inch above the flashing.

8 Install the battens to cover the gaps. Drive nails (which need to be longer than the board nails) through the gaps; avoid driving through the boards. Use a level to make sure the boards are plumb. If a batten is crooked, stretch a string alongside it and force it straight as you nail.

PANEL SIDING

Plywood panel or sheet siding offers one of the quickest and least expensive ways to cover a wall. These products have gotten a bad reputation in recent years due to reports of panels that buckle, delaminate, or come loose from the wall. But if you choose the panels and fasteners carefully and follow correct installation procedures (see Pro Tip, page 147), plywood panels can last a long time.

Cement-fiber panels are somewhat more water-repellent than plywood but should be installed with the same care as for plywood. Hardboard panels are often the least expensive option, but they are easily damaged and soak up moisture like a proverbial sponge if not kept well covered with paint at all points.

Panels are typically available in 8- and 12-foot lengths. Longer panels may enable you to minimize the number of horizontal joints between panels.

PRESTART CHECKLIST

☐ **TIME**
Working with a helper, about a day to install 1200 square feet

☐ **TOOLS**
Nail gun or hammer, circular saw, jigsaw, tape measure, story pole, chalkline, drill, flat pry bar, level, caulking gun, utility knife, tin snips, staple gun

☐ **SKILLS**
Measuring, laying out a job, driving nails, cutting with a power saw

☐ **PREP**
Cover the sheathing with building wrap and install trim boards and flashings.

☐ **MATERIALS**
Siding panels, strips of felt, staples, board and flashing for the water table, stainless-steel or galvanized siding nails, primer or sealer

1 Prepare the walls as you would for other wood sidings by applying building wrap, applying self-stick flashings at the corners and around windows and doors, and installing metal flashings as required (see pages 112–117).

2 Prime the panel edges. This is a good idea even if the panels are preprimed because plywood edges are very porous. Keep a brush and primer handy so you can prime all edges after cutting.

PANEL SIDING LAYOUT

Nails should be driven into studs. Commonly nails are placed 6 inches apart along the perimeter and 12 inches apart in the middle. Trim overlaps the siding. Use Z-flashing at any horizontal joints. Keep the panels 6 inches above grade and at least 2 inches away from concrete or asphalt stairs or walkways. Gaps may be prescribed where panels join at a shiplap joint and where plywood meets flashings.

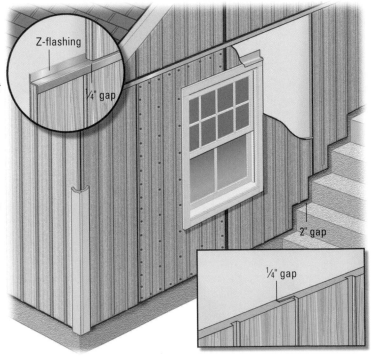

3 Locate stud centers and mark them so they can be easily transferred to the panels prior to installing (step 9). Use a level to strike a plumb line where two panels will join; marking with a lumber crayon (shown) will make the line easy to see.

4 Installation will be easier if you have a temporary ledger to rest the panels on. The ledger should be about 1 inch below the sill plate. To stabilize it pound 2×4 stakes into the ground a few inches away from the foundation. Fasten the ledger to the stakes with screws, leveling it as you go.

STANLEY PRO TIP: **Preventing damaged panels**

■ Choose high-quality panels with a proven record of durability in your area. Preprimed siding is well worth the extra cost. Look for an APA stamp guaranteeing the quality of the wood and adhesive.

■ If your studs are 16 inches on center, you can use panels rated "16 OC"; if the studs are 24 inches on center, you will need thicker sheathing rated "24 OC."

■ Install building paper, self-stick flashings, and metal flashings carefully. If moisture damage to siding is a problem in your area, consider using rain-screen methods (see page 143).

■ Prime all edges and apply two coats of primer to edges that you cut. If the siding is not preprimed, cover the backsides of the panels with primer before installing.

■ Nail into studs or other framing members, not into the sheathing alone. Use nails long enough to penetrate through the sheathing and at least 1½ inches into the framing; 8d nails are a common choice. Follow the nailing pattern recommended by the manufacturer.

■ Nailheads should be driven just tight to the wood surface. Wherever a head is sunk so it breaks the surface, fill the hole with caulk.

■ When nailing the top of a shiplap at the edge, be sure to penetrate the underlap of the abutting piece.

■ To help prevent buckling install the recommended gaps between panels and between panels and flashings (Steps 13 and 18).

5 Plan the locations of the sheets to avoid narrow slivers near the sides of windows and doors. If studs are not 16 or 24 inches on center, plan the layout carefully so all edge joints will fall over a stud. You will likely need to cut the first panel lengthwise. Measure and cut the overlap side. The underlap should extend beyond the stud so that you can nail through the overlap of the next piece.

6 Make a cutting guide for long, straight cuts. Drive screws to fasten a straight 8-foot-long 1×4 or 1×3 against the factory edge of an 8-foot-long piece of plywood that is at least 10 inches wide. Guiding the saw base on the 1×4, cut the plywood to make the cutting guide. Use the guide as shown in step 8.

7 When cutting a large panel, support it with four long boards, two on each side of the cutline. This way the panel will not fall away and possibly crack when you finish the cut.

STANLEY PRO TIP: **Measuring and snapping a chalkline**

When measuring a panel to cut to the correct width, subtract ⅛ inch to account for any gap that must occur between panels (Step 13). If you are cutting off the overlap side, measure from the face of the panel (not the underlap). Make a V-shape mark near each end of the

cut, placing the tip of the V at the precise measurement.
  Hook the chalkline at one end and pull it taut so the line crosses the V marks at their points. Pick the line straight up and let go to create a straight line.

WHAT IF...
You need to crosscut panels?

Crosscutting panels with a circular saw leaves a splintered edge on the face. To avoid this cut the sheet from the back. If you want to cut on the finish side, score the face of the panel with a utility knife just to the inside of the cutline, then cut with the circular saw.

8 Clamp the cutting guide to the siding to be cut, aligning the cut edge of the plywood part of the guide with the chalkline. Cut the siding with a circular saw, guiding the saw base along the board on the cutting guide.

9 To mark for nailing measure from a corner or the next panel to the centers of the studs. Mark the panel in three places to show where you will drive nails. If a stud is at or near a channel on the panel, you may not need to mark more than one place. (If your panels have no channels, you may choose to snap chalklines.)

10 Inside corners are rarely straight. If the corner is wavy, cut the panel 1½ inches wider than it needs to be, then hold it plumb and scribe a line along a 2×2 held against the corner. You will cover the corner with trim (Step 21), but a more accurate cut will seal better than a sloppy one.

11 Rest the sheets on the temporary ledger and check for plumb. The edge of the first sheet should be about ¼ inch shy of the corner.

12 Drive nails so they are tight and flush but do not drive the heads below the surface. It may take some practice before you can consistently drive nails without marring the panel. If you are having trouble, use a nail set when striking the last blow.

13 The ledger is handy for sliding the panel into place. With some panels you may have to temporarily tack nails in the joint to produce a ⅛-inch gap. Check with your supplier; if you neglect this gap, the panels might buckle in humid weather.

14 Hold a panel at the correct height and against a window or other obstruction to mark for the horizontal part(s) of a cutout. Cut ¼ inch above the flashing or window. Measure over from the other panel to mark the top and bottom of the vertical cut and snap a line between the marks. Again allow for a ¼-inch gap.

15 Use a circular saw to cut the lines just up to the corners and then use a jigsaw or handsaw to finish the cut.

WHAT IF...
You want a board-and-batten effect?

Create the look of board-and-batten siding (see pages 144–145) quickly and inexpensively by first applying smooth-sided plywood or fiber-cement panels (with no grooves). Use a level to install regularly spaced 1×2, 1×3, or 1×4 battens.

The joints between panels should be covered with battens; plan the layout so the joints coincide with the desired placement of battens.

16 Before installing panels above apply metal Z-flashing that overlaps onto the tops of the lower sheets. Attach the flashing by driving nails along its top edge.

17 To measure for an angle cut, hold a level so that it is plumb at each side of the sheet and measure along the level.

18 Use ¼-inch plywood spacers to create a gap between the bottoms of the upper panels and the flashing.

19 At a roofline attach flashing and install the panels 1 to 2 inches above the flashing. Use a scrap of lumber as a guide to keep the gap consistent.

20 Assemble two 1× boards to fashion trim for an outside corner and attach as shown on pages 114–115.

21 Trim inside corners with a 2×2 or a 1× board ripped to ¾ inch. Drill pilot holes to avoid splitting the wood.

REPAIRING SIDING

Holes, dents, and small areas of rot or other damage usually can be fixed quickly and inexpensively. A new generation of wood fillers, hardeners, and epoxies fill holes and firm up soft spots so they are as strong as the original wood. Metal and vinyl siding can be dented. Small repairs can add years to the life of the siding. Boards, shingles, and panels usually can be replaced without too much trouble. Often a major re-siding can be delayed by repairing sections of siding. Very likely you'll find that damage is isolated. For example wood siding on the sunny side of the house takes a beating. This chapter shows how to repair most types of siding, including stucco.

A generous coat of exterior paint will spruce up a home's appearance and protect the siding from weather and time. Though it requires only basic skills, a paint job (including preparing the walls, which is often more work than the actual painting) must be approached with careful planning and attacked with diligence and attention to detail.

Preventing serious damage

If your siding is buckling, splitting, warping, delaminating, or coming loose in large areas, or if you see mold or other signs of moisture inside the siding, remove a section and take a look. If you find plenty of moisture, the building paper and flashings may not have been installed correctly. Consult with a professional.

The solution may be as simple as caulking an opening or replacing a damaged or incorrectly installed piece of flashing. You may need to replace the felt or building paper, the flashings, and the siding, and perhaps the sheathing as well. A rain-screen installation may be indicated (see page 143).

Windows and doors present special problems. Building paper, flashings, and trim must be installed around them correctly or water can seep behind the trim and the window or door, damaging the house framing. This chapter shows the most common arrangements; for additional information see *Stanley Complete Doors & Windows*.

Most siding damage can be fixed quickly and inexpensively.

CHAPTER PREVIEW

Sealing joints
page 154

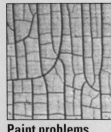
Paint problems
page 156

Prepping for house painting
page 158

Painting a house
page 160

Made for repairing
One of the advantages of lap siding is that it is relatively easy to repair. Once the nails are released and the damaged sections cut out, new pieces slip in easily. Once caulked and painted, the repair is nearly invisible.

Repairing lap siding
page 164

Repairs to other wood siding
page 166

Repairing vinyl siding
page 168

Repairing aluminum siding
page 170

Repairing stucco
page 172

SEALING JOINTS

Keeping moisture from infiltrating where it can damage sheathing and the back of siding is relatively simple. The usual problems are inadequate or poorly installed caulking around windows, doors, gable trims, and other joints. Take the time to inspect all the places where water could get in and apply high-quality caulk where needed. The exception is vinyl siding, which should be caulked only in those places where vinyl pieces abut wood or metal surfaces.

Also check your home's flashings. Read through the sections of this book that show installing your type of siding and check whether you have flashings where they are needed—above doors and windows, at vertical joints of panel or board-and-batten siding, and at the top of a water table. If you are missing some flashings, consult with a professional to see if you should remove siding pieces to install flashing or if you should simply caulk the joint well.

PRESTART CHECKLIST

☐ **TIME**
An hour or two to replace damaged flashing or apply caulk around several windows or doors

☐ **TOOLS**
Caulking gun, tin snips, lineman's pliers, flat pry bar, hammer

☐ **SKILLS**
Caulking, a skill that you can learn with 15 minutes or so of practice

☐ **PREP**
Inspect around windows, doors, and trim boards to see if you need to replace flashings or apply caulk.

☐ **MATERIALS**
High quality exterior caulk, flashings as needed, nails

Repairing flashing

1 If old galvanized flashing above a window or door is rusting or if flashing is damaged or the wrong type, pry away the top molding. Use scraps of wood to protect the window and siding as you pry.

2 Carefully pry out the siding as needed to get at the flashing underneath. Use pliers to pull out nails and then the flashing.

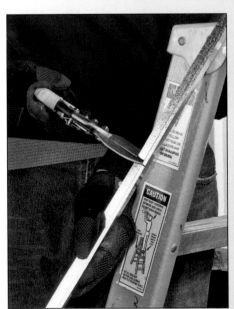

3 Use tin snips to cut new aluminum or vinyl drip-cap flashing to fit.

4 Prying away the siding as needed, slip the new flashing in place. There is no need to nail it. Replace the trim and nail the siding back down.

Applying caulk

1 Use a utility knife to cut the tip off the caulk tube. The farther from the tip you cut, the thicker the bead of caulk. Some people prefer a strongly angled cut, and others prefer one nearly perpendicular. Place the caulk tube in the gun.

2 Practice on scrap pieces if you are unsure of your skills. Hold the tube's tip against the joint, squeeze the gun's trigger, and start moving downward once caulk starts to come out. Aim for smooth motions, continually squeezing the trigger to produce smooth lines. When you get to the end, unhook the lever to stop the flow.

3 If the caulk is well adhered on both sides of the joint and the line is to your liking, you can leave it. If you want a smoother or wider line, smooth with your finger or follow the tips offered in the box, below left.

STANLEY PRO TIP: **Smoothing caulk lines**

Some people prefer to smooth caulk lines using a tool made for the purpose. Several tools are available. The one shown leaves a protective ridge of caulk.

Or use a tightly wadded rag

(above) that has been dampened with water (for latex or acrylic caulk) or mineral spirits (for oil-base caulk). You'll need to periodically rewad and clean the rag.

Caulk options

It pays in the long run to use high-quality caulk made for exterior applications. Caulk protects moisture-sensitive areas such as end grains, joints around windows and doors, corner moldings—where serious damage can occur if the wrong caulk is used. Here are some guidelines for choosing the right caulk:

■ Latex/acrylic or latex/silicone caulk is inexpensive yet fairly durable. It sticks well, is easy to work with, and is paintable. Window and door caulk is often a high-end version.

■ Butyl caulk is very durable but difficult to work with because it is very sticky. Use it where you need the best protection; have mineral-soaked rags on hand for cleanup. Gutter caulk is typically made with butyl.

■ Pure oil-base silicone caulk is very durable but may not stick to surfaces that are not completely dry and dust-free. It is also not paintable.

■ Newer versions of silicone caulk (sometimes called silicone II) have improved stickability and some are paintable.

■ To fill a wide area, use aerosol foam sealer. A "nonexpanding" version will expand a bit; "expanding" versions seem to keep growing before your eyes.

PAINT PROBLEMS

Exterior painting is a common do-it-yourself project. It typically requires little in the way of special tools and is a job that most can do successfully. However a successful paint job requires attention to detail, surface preparation, and care in selecting paint and primer. Pages 156–163 will guide you through the steps.

Start by understanding any paint problems your house may have. Applying a new coat of paint over existing paint that is peeling, blistering, or otherwise damaged will only cover things up for a year or two; the underlying problems will almost certainly reemerge. Armed with this understanding, invest the time and effort to prepare your siding and trim (pages 158–159). Then you will be ready to paint (pages 160–163).

Exterior paint should last at least 10 years, but in extreme climates the life expectancy may be shortened. Some paint problems may be simply due to years of exposure, while others are caused by poor prep work, using the wrong type of paint, or incorrect application techniques.

Blistering, peeling, or alligator skin in a small area is likely due to a specific moisture problem. For instance missing caulk or flashing may be allowing rainwater in, or a leaky gutter may be soaking the area.

Poor preparation of sheathing or siding installation can cause the siding to stay wet for long periods and lead to peeling and mildew. If this is the case with your home, a simple paint job will not solve the problem. See page 143 for more information.

Identifying paint problems

If the top coat (or perhaps two coats) is peeling but an underlying coat is sticking well, it may be that latex paint was applied over oil-base paint without first using a primer or sanding. The solution is to scrape off the top coat(s), apply a primer, and paint. If multiple coats are peeling and bare wood is showing, there may be an underlying problem causing the siding to get wet from the backside. Inspect the siding and make repairs as needed. Scrape down to bare wood, prime, and paint.

Bubbling or blistering means that moisture is trapped under the top coat, a condition that can usually be traced to bad painting technique. Paint may have been applied in hot sunlight, causing the outer skin to dry rapidly, or the underlying primer or paint may have been damp when the top coat was applied. Scrape off the blisters, sand smooth, and prime and paint while the wall is in the shade.

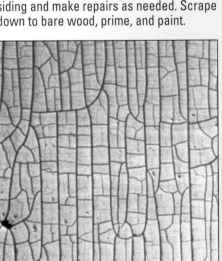

Alligator skin is usually the result of incorrect painting and priming. The top coat may be a harder paint than the underlying paint. Or a second coat may have been applied before the first had sufficient time to fully dry. Scrape off the rough skin, apply primer, and paint.

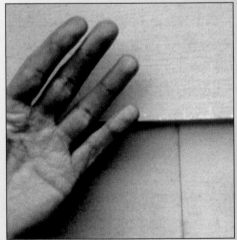

Powdery residue on your fingers when you wipe them on the surface indicates the paint is chalking. This may be caused by using cheap paint, or it may be the result of years of exposure to sun and weather. Wash the surface thoroughly with a detergent solution, prime, and paint.

Rust spots from nailheads may form splotches that flow down the wall. Sand to expose the heads and spray with rusty-metal primer, then apply regular primer and paint. Better yet remove the nails and replace them with aluminum, stainless-steel, or galvanized nails. If a metal railing shows rust, scrape with a wire brush, spray with rusty-metal primer, and paint.

Wrinkling is often the result of applying a coat of paint that is too thick. Or it can be caused by painting when the underlying coat is not yet fully dry. Sand or scrape off the wrinkles, prime, and repaint.

Damaged window glazing usually must be dealt with when painting the exterior of an older home. Old window glazing tends to crack and peel away from the glass. Scrape off the damaged glazing (a heat gun can help soften it) and apply new glazing using a putty knife that has been dipped in linseed oil.

Termite troubles

If you find meandering channels running through wood trim or siding (usually just below the surface), you may have a wood-boring insect infestation. Another telltale sign is the presence of "mud tubes," small covered bridges running along the foundation up to the siding. Call several professional pest control companies for assessments and prices.

Termites typically live in the ground outside and make daily forays into the home to dine on wood fibers. They are happy eating dry wood since they can get moisture back at the ranch. The solution is to drill a series of holes outside (sometimes through a concrete walk or driveway) and inject poison to kill the queen and the rest of the colony. A pest control company may return regularly to inject poison into the holes, or they may install a barrier to keep the wood-eaters out.

Carpenter ants usually live in the place where they dine and are attracted to wet wood. The solution is usually to kill the ants with insecticide, then take steps to keep the wood dry.

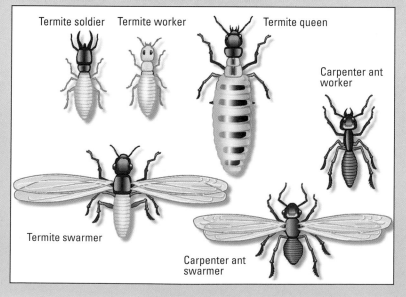

PREPPING FOR HOUSE PAINTING

Proper surface preparation is essential to a successful paint job, so don't skimp on time or elbow grease. Depending on the condition of the siding and trim, you may spend much more time preparing for painting than actually applying the paint.

The ideal surface for a good appearance is smooth yet slightly roughed up so the paint can adhere. In cases of severe damage or heavy paint buildup, you need the ultimate approach: Scrape and sand down to bare wood. A more moderate approach is usually enough: Sand the paint smooth and apply primer. If the existing surface is in good condition, you can get by with washing, spot-sanding, and priming.

Rotted areas can be hardened and holes filled, but if the area is large, you may want to simply replace the boards.

PRESTART CHECKLIST

☐ **TIME**
You can wash 300 square feet in 1 hour or less. Scraping down to bare wood may take weeks.

☐ **TOOLS**
Pressure washer, paint scrapers, power paint remover, sanding blocks, power sander, heat gun, paintbrush, wire brush, steel wool, putty knife, abrasive pads, caulking gun, utility knife, ladders and/or scaffolding

☐ **SKILLS**
Elbow grease and patient attention to detail

☐ **PREP**
Protect plantings and lawn with drop cloths.

☐ **MATERIALS**
Sandpaper, liquid or paste paint remover, caulk, wood filler, wood hardener, epoxy filler, glazing putty

Repairing rotted wood

1 Scrape away any loose material, but you can leave soft rotted wood in place. If the area is wet, dry it out before proceeding. Drill a series of holes wherever you suspect the wood may be rotted beneath the surface. Apply wood hardener to all the rotted wood.

2 Allow the hardener to dry. If the hole is deep, partially fill with scraps of wood. Mix a batch of two-part epoxy filler.

3 If needed tack on a rough form to hold the epoxy. Continue filling and pressing until the area is slightly overfilled. Use a putty knife or a scraping tool to roughly mold the filler to the shape of the surrounding wood. You may be able to cut a plastic scraper to the desired profile.

4 The epoxy will start to harden quickly. While it is hard but not yet dry, scrape to get the basic shape. Once it has dried finish the shaping using a sanding block or handheld piece of sandpaper.

Preparing siding

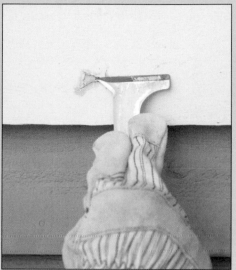

Many walls can be prepared simply by cleaning with a stiff brush (perhaps a push broom on a large area of siding). Use a mild detergent solution, then rinse thoroughly. Or use a pressure washer as shown. Spray with a fan nozzle and avoid getting too close or you may damage the wood.

Use a pull-type scraper with replaceable blades to remove paint from small areas. Press down on the blade with one hand as you pull with the other. When a blade becomes dull, replace or sharpen it.

At corners and on molded trim, use a detail scraper, which comes with a selection of variously shaped curved and pointed blades. If dry-scraping makes for slow progress, apply paste paint stripper according to instructions, wait for the paint to bubble, and scrape. Wear protective clothing when working with chemicals and keep a bucket handy for collecting scrapings.

Remove small amounts of paint and smooth a scraped area using a power sander. Periodically knock the dust out of the sandpaper and change the paper when needed. Or use a drywall-type sander on a pole.

A rotary power paint remover like this can remove all the paint in a fairly short amount of time. It will reach up to an edge but cannot get into a corner. Make sure it has a dust collector and empty it regularly.

Another paint removing tool applies intense heat to a small area so you can quickly scrape away the paint. This can reach into corners.

SAFETY FIRST
Take care with
lead paint

Older paint may contain lead, which is a health hazard. Use a home testing kit to find out if your paint contains lead or have a building inspector check it out. If you have lead paint, leave it in place and paint over it; scraping or sanding will release airborne particles that are very harmful if inhaled. Or pay a licensed company to remove it.

PAINTING A HOUSE

Before painting, take time to prepare the surfaces and fill any gaps at joints with caulk (page 155). Allow a day or so for the caulk to dry completely before you apply paint over it.

If your existing surface is in good shape and the new paint will be close to the same color, you can simply apply paint and skip priming. In many cases, however, at least spot-priming is recommended. Good primer seals bare wood, ensures that the new paint will adhere to the old paint, and keeps stains from bleeding through. A reputable paint dealer will not charge for tinting the primer so it is close to the color of the paint you will apply.

Today's acrylic paint is as durable as oil-base paint when applied to siding and trim. It sticks better and lasts longer than less expensive latex paints.

Buy high-quality brushes and roller sleeves made for the type of paint you will be using. Good tools apply paint thicker and smoother, and this can make the difference between needing one coat or two.

Priming

1 Use a putty knife or scraper to fill small holes with exterior spackle, which dries quickly. Sand smooth.

2 Apply primer using a brush, roller, or sprayer. Follow the techniques for painting described in the following steps. Allow the primer to dry fully before applying paint.

PRESTART CHECKLIST

☐ **TIME**
Using a brush on a house with lap siding and wood trim, a day to prime or paint about 1,500 square feet

☐ **TOOLS**
Putty knife, paintbrushes, rollers and sleeves, airless sprayer, ladders and/or scaffolding

☐ **SKILLS**
Careful and accurate painting can be learned as you go.

☐ **PREP**
Protect plants and the lawn with drop cloths.

☐ **MATERIALS**
Exterior spackle, primer, paint, bucket, masking tape, cleaning fluids (if using alkyd- or oil-base paint), rags

STANLEY PRO TIP

The order of work

Paint when the weather is 50°F or warmer with no threat of rain. Paint in the shade; painting on a wall exposed to direct sunlight can cause blisters. You may be able to follow the shade around the house.

On a house with beveled siding or shingles that butt up to trim, it is usually easiest to paint the trim first, then the siding. With panel and other types of siding, it may be easiest to paint the siding first. Experiment painting a corner to see which line is easiest to paint accurately and paint that last. In general start at the top—the eaves and fascia—and work down.

Loading a brush

Pour paint into an oversize bucket, so you won't have to worry about spilling a full-to-the-brim pail. When painting a large area, dip the brush about 2 inches into the paint, then slap the brush lightly against the bucket on both sides. When painting a straight line along the edge of trim, dip only an inch or so and scrape off one side of the paint on the bucket's rim.

Brush-painting siding

1 Brush a generous amount of paint into the corners and make sure the corners are filled. Even if the trim or siding (depending which you paint first) will be painted a different color, don't worry about lapping onto the trim; filling the corners is the important thing.

2 Apply a generous amount of paint to the siding. Finish with a long, light stroke to produce a smooth surface.

Painting trim and windows

Scrape paint off one side of the brush and press the loaded side against the trim about 1 inch away from the edge where you need to paint a straight line. Brush toward the line and paint the line slowly but with a smooth stroke. Once the line is painted, move on to the faces of the trim. When painting a window slide the sashes ajar; paint and periodically slide the sashes while the paint dries.

Using a roller

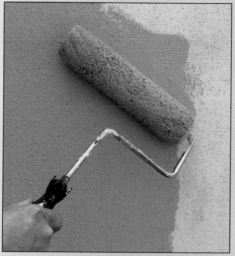

Use a medium-nap roller sleeve when painting siding. Brush-paint the corners first, then use the roller. A 3-inch roller sleeve sometimes speeds up the painting of trim—worth doing before siding.

When painting stucco or rough-textured siding, use a roller sleeve with a nap that is ¾ inch or thicker.

Using masking tape

Some people prefer to paint lines using masking or painter's tape. Carefully press the tape with your finger or fingernail to make sure it adheres tightly so no paint can sneak behind. Apply paint that laps onto the tape and carefully pull the tape straight back and away while the paint is still wet.

Painting with a sprayer

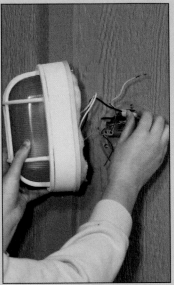

1 Cut pieces of plastic sheeting or rosin paper to fit over windows and doors; attach with painter's tape. You may need to apply additional tape to accurately mask the paint lines at the edges. If the trim will be differently colored than the walls, either spray the walls first, then handpaint the trim (if the lines between trim and wall are not straight) or paint the trim, mask the trim, then spray the walls (if the lines are straight).

2 Mask receptacles, spigots, and other fixtures. Wrap the tape tightly and accurately around the perimeter to create clean lines. Press firmly on the tape so paint cannot seep underneath.

3 Wrap light fixtures with plastic or rosin paper and carefully tape the edges. Better yet remove the fixtures before painting.

Choosing a sprayer

A professional-quality airless sprayer can be rented, unless you expect to paint often. Look for a unit with wheels so you can easily move it around. It should have a long hose and the gun should feel comfortable in your hand. Ask the rental salesperson about cleanup; the unit should have a good track record for staying unclogged and there should be only a few nozzle parts to clean. There will likely be a pressure control dial that you can adjust. Better sprayers have a reversible spray tip, which allows you to quickly unclog it without having to dismantle parts. Check to see if the manufacturer recommends

thinning or straining paint. Some units, like the one shown here, have a hopper that you fill with paint; others have a hose that runs into a 5-gallon bucket of paint, which may fit onto the unit's cart so you can easily wheel it around.

WHAT IF...
You buy an inexpensive sprayer?

For about $100 you can buy a sprayer that may suit your needs. It will work more slowly than a higher end unit and you may need to stop and clean the parts every few hours, but the results can be professional-looking. Paint must be strained and thinned, using a testing strip or cup that comes with the sprayer to measure viscosity. Use the unit's plastic canister when painting small areas. For larger areas, some sprayers let you run a hose into a bucket of paint.

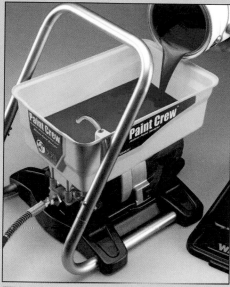

4 Connect the sprayer's hose to the motor and to the gun as directed by the manufacturer. Plug in the cord.

5 Load the hopper or bucket with paint. Some sprayers recommend that you strain the paint, using straining cloths that fit over the bucket or hopper. You may need to thin the paint as well.

6 Follow instructions for priming the unit and perhaps also purging the lines of any paint left over from a previous job. You will need to point the gun at a practice surface, such as a sheet of plywood. Use this opportunity to practice your spraying technique.

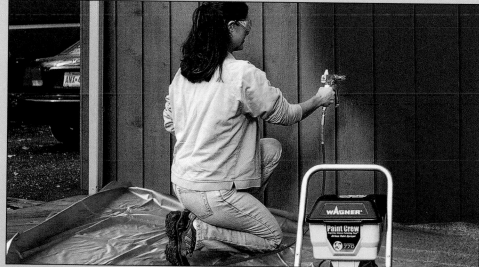

7 The spray should be a fine mist. It should cover a fairly wide area, applying paint with even thickness at all points. Start by spraying at a slight angle against moldings and other masked obstructions so you get into the corners. Always keep the sprayer moving. When you spray a large wall area, keep the nozzle pointed straight at the wall at all times; move the sprayer from side to side, rather than turning it at an angle. If the sprayer starts to spit globs, stop and clear the nozzle. This may be as simple as reversing the nozzle and spraying briefly. If you spray too heavily, you will make globs or runs. Stop painting and smooth these with a large brush or roller.

8 When you stop for a break or at the end of the job, clean the nozzle immediately. It may work to simply replace the paint with slightly soapy water and then shoot the water for a minute or so. You may need to disassemble the nozzle and place the parts in a small bucket of water or solvent. Clean with a small brush and rinse.

REPAIRING LAP SIDING

If a wood clapboard is rotted in a small area, you can apply wood hardener and patch with wood filler or epoxy. If the damaged area is large, you'll have to replace the board or a part of the board. You can cut a board most anywhere if your sheathing is solid plywood or OSB, but if the sheathing is not solid, it must be cut in the middle of a stud so the joint can be firmly nailed.

If there is widespread rotting, the area behind may be getting wet and the problem may be with the building paper or the way the siding was installed. See page 143 for more information.

Siding that is buckling or pulling away from the wall may be insufficiently nailed. Try driving longer nails or screws into studs.

Beveled siding made of pressed board, which is no longer made, is notoriously unstable and weak. If yours is warping, buckling, or flaking apart, it needs to be removed and replaced.

PRESTART CHECKLIST

☐ **TIME**
Less than an hour for most repairs

☐ **TOOLS**
Hammer, tape measure, square, flat pry bar, putty knife, Surform tool, keyhole saw, caulking gun, paintbrush, sanding block, utility knife

☐ **SKILLS**
Cutting, measuring, fastening

☐ **PREP**
Check the siding closely for further damage to determine how large a section of siding needs to be replaced.

☐ **MATERIALS**
Wood filler, wood hardener, caulk, exterior or polyurethane glue, nails or screws, roofing felt, sandpaper, primer and paint

Filling holes

Fill small holes (like those made by screws that have been removed) with exterior caulk. Smooth with a putty knife, allow to dry, and paint.

For larger holes or for dents or gaps at joints, use exterior wood filler. Slightly overfill and smooth with a putty knife, then sand once the filler is dry. Or use epoxy filler, as shown on page 158.

Repairing a split

1 Using a chisel or putty knife, gently pry open a split and squirt in exterior wood glue or polyurethane glue.

2 Drill upward-angled pilot holes and drive small-headed stainless-steel screws to tighten the crack. If the sheathing is not solid plywood or OSB, you may need to temporarily screw a board over the area and remove the board when the glue dries.

Replacing siding pieces

1 If the siding board above has exposed nails that go into the board that you want to remove, pry away the siding board above and then tap it back in. The nailheads should pull out to the point where you can grab and remove them with a pry bar. Tap in shims to hold the board away from the wall. You will probably need to do this for a fairly wide area on each side of the damage. Pry out the nails holding the damaged siding. If you are removing an entire board, pull out all the nails and then pry out the board.

2 To cut out a damaged area, use a square and a utility knife to scribe cutlines on each side of the damage. Using a circular saw set to the thickness of the siding, complete as much of the cut as you can without cutting into the siding above the cut. Be careful not to damage the sheathing.

3 Using a scrap of wood as a guide, finish the cuts with a keyhole saw. Measure or use the cutouts as templates. Cut replacement siding boards to fit. If the building paper is damaged, see page 166 for repair instructions.

4 Tap the new pieces in place, using a block of wood so you don't dent the siding. Drill pilot holes and drive nails to attach the new pieces. Remove the shims and tap the upper board back into place. Caulk the joints. Apply primer and paint.

REPAIRS TO OTHER WOOD SIDING

Dents and holes in panel or board-and-batten siding can be repaired with exterior wood filler, caulk, or epoxy filler (page 158). If a panel is delaminating, it should be removed and replaced. Siding that is coming away from the wall or buckling may simply need to be reattached with longer nails or screws, preferably driven into studs. Battens require very long nails.

If there is widespread rotting, the area behind may be getting wet, and the problem may be with the building paper or the way the siding was installed. See page 143 for more information.

Panels that are made of hardboard are easily cracked and very susceptible to water damage. They are usually impossible to repair, so replace them instead.

Read the sections of this book that show installing your type of siding to make sure it is correctly attached.

PRESTART CHECKLIST

☐ **TIME**
Less than an hour for most repairs

☐ **TOOLS**
Hammer, tape measure, level, square, flat pry bar, putty knife, chisel, hacksaw blade, nail set, caulking gun, paintbrush, utility knife

☐ **SKILLS**
Cutting, measuring, fastening

☐ **PREP**
Check the siding closely for further damage to determine how large a section of siding needs to be replaced.

☐ **MATERIALS**
Wood filler, wood hardener, caulk, exterior or polyurethane glue, roofing felt or building paper, nails or screws, sandpaper, primer and paint

Board-and-batten

1 Boards and battens can usually be removed easily with a hammer and a flat pry bar. Use a scrap of wood or a shim to protect adjoining boards. To remove a board first remove the battens on both sides of it.

2 Paint the back and sides of the replacement board with primer or sealer. Use shims to maintain gaps of at least ¼ inch on either side, then drive nails to attach. Use a level and/or string line to keep the battens straight as you nail them in place.

STANLEY PRO TIP: **Keeping the sheathing covered**

1 If the felt or building paper is damaged, staple it back down smoothly or cut the damage away.

2 Cut a piece of felt as large as possible and slip it under the boards above and on the sides. Staple the patch, then replace the siding.

Shingles

1 Use a hammer and chisel to split apart a damaged siding shingle. Try to split the shingle at or near a nail in the piece above.

2 Use pliers or your hands to wiggle and pull the pieces out.

3 Use a hacksaw blade or a detail hacksaw tool to cut through hidden nails above. Flex the blade to cut the nail flush with the wall.

4 Reassemble the damaged shingle to make a template for cutting the replacement shingle. Or measure the area and subtract about ¼ inch to allow for expansion. Cut with a knife or a saw.

5 Slide the replacement up until it is ½ inch below its final position. Just under the course above, drive two nails at slight upward angles. Use a nail set to finish driving the nails.

6 Use a scrap of wood and a hammer to tap the replacement shingle up, aligned with the shingles on either side.

REPAIRING VINYL SIDING

If a vinyl piece has come apart from its neighbor, the solution is often to push it back up until it locks in place (see Step 5 on page 169).

If many of the pieces are coming apart or buckling, they may have been installed with nails driven tightly; nails should be loose so the material can expand and contract. If that is the case, you may need to remove the siding from an area and reinstall it (see pages 130–135).

If you need to replace a vinyl panel or part of a panel, check your garage or basement to see whether the installer left extra pieces for repairs. Otherwise take a sample to a siding supplier and look for a close match.

Even if you find an exact replacement, the siding on your walls may have faded, meaning that the new pieces will be noticeably darker. If the repair is on a highly visible portion of the house, you may want to remove a piece from a less-visible part of the house (perhaps in the back or behind a bush) and use that as the patch; then install the recently bought piece at the less-visible location.

PRESTART CHECKLIST

☐ **TIME**
Less than an hour for most repairs

☐ **TOOLS**
Hammer, tape measure, zipper tool, flat pry bar, tin snips, utility knife, caulking gun

☐ **SKILLS**
Simple cutting and measuring skills

☐ **PREP**
Check the siding closely for further damage to determine how large a section of siding needs to be replaced.

☐ **MATERIALS**
Replacement siding panels, butyl caulk (or gutter caulk), duct tape, materials for bracing a patch temporarily

Patching a small area

1 Use a utility knife to cut around the damaged area. If possible leave at least 2 inches of siding along the top edge of the damaged piece. Use a zipper tool (page 169) to remove the cutout.

2 Use a square and a utility knife to cut a patch piece that is about 4 inches wider than the area you cut out. Slice off the nailing strip or upper part of the patch.

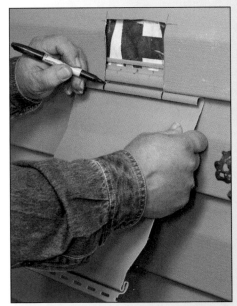

3 Mark and cut away the side portions of the snap-in flange. Test the patch for fit; it should just slip under the piece above once it has been snapped into place at the bottom.

4 Apply a generous bead of butyl caulk all around the cutout. Press the patch into place and push up to snap it in place. Use a temporary brace or duct tape to hold the patch in place for about a day. Remove the brace or tape once the caulk has dried.

Replacing a panel section

1 Use a zipper tool to pry out the panel above the one you want to remove. Slip shims all along the disassembled joint.

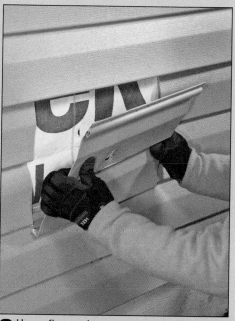

2 Use a square and a knife to cut through the panel on one or both sides of the damage. Cut carefully so you do not damage the building paper underneath.

3 Use a flat pry bar to remove the nails and the damaged section of siding. Cut a replacement panel that is 4 inches longer than the damaged section.

4 Apply generous beads of butyl (or gutter) caulk on the adjacent siding about ½ inch from the edges of the cutout area.

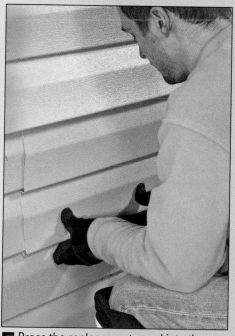

5 Press the replacement panel into the caulk and slide it up. Press on the bottom to snap it in place.

6 Remove the shims and use a zipper tool to snap it onto the flange of the replacement panel. Press the panel into the caulk, making sure that it seals at all points.

REPAIRING ALUMINUM SIDING

Most aluminum siding joins together much like vinyl. Patch a damaged area or replace a panel following the instructions on pages 168–169.

Metal corner caps are sometimes used instead of corner posts for aluminum siding, and in older installations they were often used for wood or hardboard lap siding as well. If your local supplier does not have caps to match the ones on your house, check online sources; it helps if you know the manufacturer's name. In a pinch you can cut and shape a piece of sheet metal to fit, using an old cap as a template.

Aluminum siding can and should be painted. Scrape any flaking paint, and sand smooth. Pressure-wash and allow to dry. Apply an alcohol-base primer, or an oil-base primer that has been thinned with 2 cups of thinner per gallon of primer. Apply acrylic paint.

PRESTART CHECKLIST

☐ **TIME**
Less than an hour for most repairs

☐ **TOOLS**
Hammer, tape measure, pliers, putty knife, nail set, linemen's pliers, taping blade, flat pry bar, tin snips, hacksaw, sanding block, caulking gun, ladder

☐ **SKILLS**
Simple cutting and measuring skills

☐ **PREP**
Check the siding closely for further damage to determine how large a section of siding needs to be replaced.

☐ **MATERIALS**
Butyl (gutter) caulk, replacement end caps, auto-body filler, scraper, sandpaper

Corner caps

1 To remove damaged caps gently pry out the siding, pry out the caps at their bottoms, and pull with pliers. If that doesn't work you may need to cut at the top with a hacksaw as shown. Take care to cut only through the cap and not into the siding. Wood siding is shown, but caps on aluminum siding are similar.

2 Use pliers to remove nails or use a nail set to pound them in. Insert the new corner caps. Where the top of a cap is exposed, drive nails to attach. Use a nail set to finish driving.

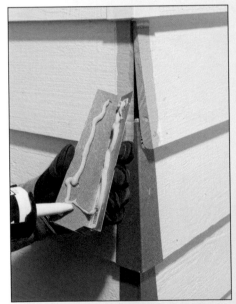

3 Where you cannot drive nails (typical on the topmost cap), test to make sure you can slip a cap under the siding above. Apply butyl (gutter) caulk to the backside of the cap.

4 Press the glued cap in place and use tape to hold it until the caulk dries. Remove the tape after a day. Prime and paint.

Small patch

1 Tap with a hammer to indent the damaged area or use tin snips or a utility knife to cut it out.

2 Cut a patch 4 inches longer than the damage and cut off the nailing flange. Test the fit; the patch should just slip under the siding above.

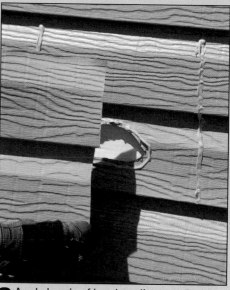

3 Apply beads of butyl caulk on each side of the patch area and around the hole. Press the patch into place. Use duct tape to hold it in place while the caulk dries.

Filling a dent

1 If a dent is deep, partially drive a coarse-threaded screw into the center and pull it partway out with a pair of pliers. If part of the damaged area protrudes, tap with a hammer to indent it slightly.

2 Scrape and sand away any loose paint. Clean with a mild detergent solution, rinse, and allow to dry thoroughly. Mix a batch of autobody filler and apply it over the indentation, using the plastic scraper that comes with the filler.

3 When it gets hard but not dry, generally shape the filler with a scraper. When it dries use a hand sander to smooth the patch. Prime and paint.

REPAIRING STUCCO

On a wood-sheathed stucco wall, the sheathing is covered with roofing felt, then wire lath is nailed over the felt. Two or three layers of stucco are applied over the lath. On a masonry wall stucco is typically applied directly with no lath.

Before patching a small area, press hard with your palm against the surrounding wall. Wherever you find sponginess the stucco has disengaged from the wall and should be removed and replaced.

Getting a stucco patch to blend with its surroundings is more difficult than it may first appear. However by experimenting with various tools, you can likely discover how to apply a texture that comes close (for options, see the box on page 173).

PRESTART CHECKLIST

☐ **TIME**
An hour or less for a small patch (not including drying time); several days for a large patch

☐ **TOOLS**
Caulking gun, hammer, cold chisel, wire brush, lineman's pliers, tin snips, putty knife, old can opener, detail scraper, masonry brush, magnesium float or flat trowel, scarifying tool, paint roller, wheelbarrow or trough, masonry hoe, ladder or scaffolding

☐ **SKILLS**
Measuring, laying out a job, driving nails, cutting with a knife

☐ **PREP**
Protect plants and the lawn with a drop cloth or plastic sheeting.

☐ **MATERIALS**
Stucco caulk or exterior caulk, stucco patch, stucco mix (basecoat and finish), roofing felt, stucco lath, roofing nails

Small holes

1 Tap with a hammer and chisel to remove any loose stucco. Use a wire brush, then a wet bristle brush, to clean out dust and debris.

2 If needed nail in place a new piece of mesh. Dampen the area with a wet rag shortly before applying the patch.

3 Use a putty knife or trowel to apply a ready-mix stucco patch. It may take two or three layers to fill the hole. Allow each layer to dry before applying the next.

4 When you reach the last layer, use one of the techniques shown on page 173 to match the texture. Here a brush is used in a sweeping, semicircular motion.

Cracks

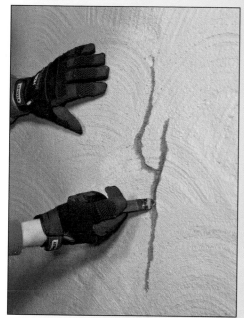

1 Use an old puncture can opener or a detail paint scraper to dig out and widen the crack. Work to make the innermost part of the crack wider than the surface crack.

2 Apply stucco or mortar caulk, both of which have a grainy texture that blends with a stucco wall. Or to seal but not texture the crack, use regular exterior caulk (see page 155).

see page 155

STANLEY PRO TIP

Tinting and painting stucco

Some stucco is pigmented with integral colorant. To match an existing color, buy pigment from a masonry supply source and test a number of recipes, keeping track of the ratio of pigment to stucco. The color will change as the stucco dries. This is difficult so you may choose to paint the wall instead.

Wait for the stucco to completely dry; this may take several days or even a week.

Use a thick-napped roller or a sprayer to apply a high-quality primer, then cover this with elastomeric paint made for stucco and masonry surfaces. Acrylic paint also works well.

WHAT IF...
You need to texture your patch?

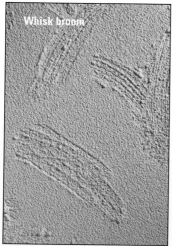
Whisk broom

Scallops

Spatter

Knockdown

Start with a basically smooth wall that is at the same thickness as the surrounding surfaces. Use a masonry brush or a **whisk broom** to etch swirls, straight lines, or a

pattern of alternating straight lines. You may need to periodically rinse the brush in a bucket of water.

To make a series of **scallops,** use a triangular trowel, sculpting

with a semicircular motion.

To produce a **spatter** texture, dip a brush in a bucket of fairly wet stucco mix and flick at the wall by tapping the brush against

a small scrap of wood.

To create a **knockdown** texture, start with peaks created by pulling back and gently smooth the surface with a trowel.

GUTTERS AND EAVES

The area below a roof overhang—gutter and eave territory—is a common trouble spot. This chapter will guide you through repairs to fascia and soffits as well as show you how to repair and install new gutters.

Water running off the roof should flow over the roofing, then over the drip-edge flashing and directly into gutters and down the downspouts. When everything is working the fascia and roof sheathing will stay relatively dry. However in an imperfect world, flashings may be poorly installed, roofing may fail, and gutters may overflow or leak. Any of these conditions can soak the fascia, the soffits, and perhaps the ends of rafters and roof sheathing as well.

If you see signs of damage to your eaves, run a hose on the roof to check that the drip-edge flashing and gutters are installed correctly, so that water flows into the gutter and does not seep into the sheathing or fascia. While the water is running, watch the gutter and downspouts for leaks and make needed repairs. Also check that the roofing is sound (see pages 84–85) and make any needed repairs or replacements. If ice dams (see page 84) form during the winter, they are likely the culprit; take steps to ventilate the attic or otherwise protect against the dams.

You will likely need to remove the gutters to repair or replace fascia and soffit boards. If the gutters are in less than excellent condition, this may be the time to replace them. If boards are only water-stained or if rot is only in small spots, you may choose to apply wood hardener and epoxy filler (see page 158). If the damage is deep or wide, replace all or part of the board.

Whenever you remove a board, take time to check for further damage underneath it. If the area is wet, allow it to dry thoroughly before proceeding. If rafter ends are slightly rotted, you may be able to solve the problem by applying wood hardener. Otherwise it may be necessary to cut the ends short and perhaps to add reinforcing "sister" pieces alongside. Use pressure-treated lumber when replacing any wood pieces.

Here's how to keep water safely flowing off and away from the roof.

CHAPTER PREVIEW

Fascia and soffit repairs
page 176

Gutter repairs
page 178

Installing gutters
page 182

Get help
It's possible to hang gutters by yourself, but the job is made much easier with an extra pair of hands. Dry-fitting sections will spare you from climbing up and down ladders.

Vinyl gutter systems are readily available, easy to cut, and straightforward to install. Plan your project and list all the components you need but buy extra pieces to allow for the unexpected.

FASCIA AND SOFFIT REPAIRS

Along the eaves you will often find fascia boards covering the ends of roof rafters as well as soffit boards (or sheets of plywood, aluminum, or vinyl) covering the underside of the eaves (see the illustration below). A gutter usually is attached to the fascia (see pages 178–185 for gutter repairs and installation).

Fascia boards can get soaked with rainwater if the drip-edge flashing is damaged or incorrectly installed or if the roofing itself fails. If this leads to rot, fascia boards need to be replaced. This does not call for special skills, but the work can be a bit messy. Be sure to work on a stable ladder or scaffolding and be careful not to lean too far to one side of the ladder while you work.

Replace old boards with pressure-treated 1× lumber or plywood. It doesn't cost much more than untreated wood and it will help prevent rot.

PRESTART CHECKLIST

☐ **TIME**
Several hours to replace a fascia board; more time if other repairs are needed

☐ **TOOLS**
Flat pry bar, tape measure, circular saw, reciprocating saw, keyhole saw, T-bevel, string line, drill, hammer, paintbrush

☐ **SKILLS**
Basic carpentry

☐ **PREP**
Remove the gutters and inspect the roof.

☐ **MATERIALS**
Galvanized nails or deck screws, boards or plywood to match the damaged materials, soffit materials, caulk, primer, paint

Repairing fascia

1 Remove an entire board or cut alongside a rafter with a reciprocating saw to remove the damaged portion of a board. Pry the fascia away using a flat pry bar and a hammer. Take care not to dent the soffit or other boards while you pry. You likely will need to pry out the bottom first, then pry the board down from the roof. Pull out or pound in any exposed nails.

2 If the board meets another board in the center of a rafter, you can attach the new board in the same way. For greater strength cut a short 2×6 or 2×4 and install it alongside the rafter to provide more nailing surface. Attach with deck screws.

EAVE ANATOMY

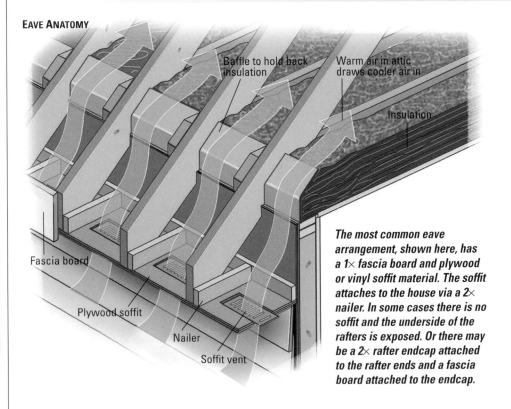

Baffle to hold back insulation

Warm air in attic draws cooler air in

Insulation

Fascia board

Plywood soffit

Nailer

Soffit vent

The most common eave arrangement, shown here, has a 1× fascia board and plywood or vinyl soffit material. The soffit attaches to the house via a 2× nailer. In some cases there is no soffit and the underside of the rafters is exposed. Or there may be a 2× rafter endcap attached to the rafter ends and a fascia board attached to the endcap.

3 Check for further rot (see Pro Tip at right) and replace the drip edge if needed (see page 92). Near the top of where the replacement board will go, attach a taut string to use as a guide for straightness. Cut a new fascia piece to fit. Tap it up into position (if it is long have a helper hold the other end) and attach it to the rafter ends with nails or screws.

WHAT IF...
You choose a scarf joint?

A scarf joint is a good idea if the fascia is highly visible, and you may need to match an existing scarf joint. This is typically done by cutting the board at a 45-degree bevel, but 22½-degree bevels are also used. Cut a scrap piece to make sure the angle is right. Drill pilot holes before driving nails.

STANLEY PRO TIP

Dealing with rot in soffits, sheathing, and rafter ends

If the roofing or flashing has failed, more than just the fascia may be damaged. The roof sheathing, soffit boards, and even rafters may have rotted as well. After removing the fascia poke all the exposed wood with a screwdriver; if the tip sinks in easily, the board is rotted. If the rot on a board is only half an inch or so deep, it's usually okay to leave the board in place. Dry the area out and replace any other boards and flashings as needed to keep the area dry.

If several rafter ends are rotted, you may need to uniformly trim 2 inches or so from them. Work carefully so they will all be the same length and angle. Or install "sister" 2× boards alongside the rafters and attach the fascia and soffit to the sisters.

For sheathing repairs see pages 38–39.

Soffit repairs

1 If a portion of a soffit is damaged, draw a straight line alongside the framing (nailheads will likely show you where framing members are) and cut with a reciprocating saw or hand keyhole saw. Or remove the entire board (which will be no longer than 8 feet if it is plywood).

2 Pry out any molding covering the edges of the soffit board. Use a flat pry bar, then your hands, to pull out the damaged board. Inspect the exposed boards for further rot.

3 Use the old piece as a template for cutting a new piece. You may choose to add soffit vents at this time (see page 98). Attach the new soffit piece with screws or nails and replace any moldings.

GUTTER REPAIRS

For a gutter system to efficiently carry water away, it must be free of holes or loose joints, sloped at all points toward the downspouts, and clear of debris (usually leaves) that can slow the flow and clog downspouts.

Regularly clean out your gutters using a small trowel, a special plastic gutter-cleaning tool, or a gloved hand. Cut back branches that drop leaves and twigs onto the roof. Install gutter guards (see below).

When inspecting gutters up close, check for rotted fascia boards or sheathing and make repairs as shown on pages 38–39 and 176–177. Also make sure the drip-edge flashing is properly installed (page 92), so rain flows into the gutter and not onto the fascia or the edge of the sheathing.

Vinyl gutters are reliable, though the joints may come loose. Galvanized steel gutters will rust in time and need to be patched or have sections replaced. Aluminum gutters are rustproof but easily dented.

A gutter may be attached using brackets, spikes, or a strap. Each type can loosen, especially if the fascia rots. All attachment parts can be easily replaced.

Work on a stable ladder or scaffolding and avoid leaning far over while working.

PRESTART CHECKLIST

☐ **TIME**
With materials in hand, less than an hour

☐ **TOOLS**
Flat pry bar, hacksaw or power saw, caulking gun, pop riveter, putty knife, stiff brush, garden hose, drill, hammer

☐ **SKILLS**
Basic carpentry, working at heights

☐ **PREP**
Inspect during a rainfall for drips or overflowing water. Clean out debris. Test that gutters are firmly attached.

☐ **MATERIALS**
Replacement gutter parts to match, gutter caulk, roofing cement, patching materials, pop rivets

Unclogging downspouts

If water runs sluggishly or not at all through a downspout, try flushing it with a garden hose. If you need more pressure, seal the gap around the hose with a tightly stuffed rag.

If a hose doesn't do the trick, try running a plumbing auger—either a hand-crank model or a power auger—down the downspout. The auger may push the obstruction through or it may pull debris back out. As a last resort dismantle the downspout (page 180) and clear out the sections individually.

STANLEY PRO TIP: **Gutter guards**

Several manufacturers offer gutter covers—often claiming that their product is the only one that really works. There are two basic options. A screen guard (above) keeps out all large debris; some models are smooth and sloped so the leaves can slide over the gutter. A solid cover (above right) has an opening at the front that allows only flowing water into the gutter. Whichever type you choose test by directing a hose onto the roof to be sure the water will flow into the gutter and not slip behind, where it can damage sheathing or fascia.

Patching a hole

1 For a sturdy repair cut a piece of metal flashing several inches wider and longer than the hole. Use a putty knife to bend it so it conforms to the shape of the gutter.

2 Spread a generous coat of roofing cement onto the inside of the gutter and press the sheet metal into the cement. Cover the metal with more cement and feather the edges so that water can flow easily over it.

WHAT IF...
You use a patch kit?

Self-stick patching material is quick to apply but may not be a permanent solution. Brush the area free of dust and debris, then follow the manufacturer's application instructions.

Sealing joints and caps

If the gutter drips at a downspout or joint, you may be able to simply seal the leak with gutter caulk. First check that the joint is firm and drive screws or rivets if needed. Apply a generous bead of caulk, then smooth the caulk with a wood shim or a balled-up, mineral spirit-dampened rag.

If an endcap has come loose, remove any screws and pull off the cap. Replace the cap if it is not in sound condition. Apply caulk to the inside grooves and press it back into place.

Drive screws or pop rivets if called for. Caulk the inside of the endcap as well.

Sealing downspouts

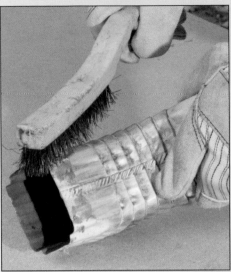

1 If a downspout joint leaks, check to be sure the male (smaller) end of the upper piece is slid into the female (larger) end of the lower piece. To dismantle the parts remove any screws or drill out pop rivets. You'll probably need to remove a wall bracket as well. Pull apart the pieces.

2 If a part is badly bent or otherwise damaged, replace it. If it is basically in good shape, clean off any old caulk and grime with a wire brush.

3 Apply a generous bead of caulk to the male portion of the upper piece. Slip the other piece over the caulk and drive screws or pop rivets to firmly attach the joint. Add a touch of caulk to the outside of the joint.

Fixing the slope

A gutter should be sloped at a rate of 1/16 inch per foot or 1/2 inch over an 8-foot span. Test by directing a hose into the gutter and watching the water or use a level.

If the gutter is supported by straps, install new straps as needed. Slip the strap onto the gutter and raise the gutter to the correct position. Drive screws to attach the strap.

If a spike-and-ferrule system is used, position a ferrule (sleeve) at a rafter (don't just attach to the fascia) and drill a hole in the front of the gutter. Drive a spike or long deck screw through the ferrule and into the fascia and rafter end.

Replacing a section

1 If a gutter is installed in 8- or 10-foot sections, it is usually best to unfasten the screws or drill out the pop rivets and remove an entire section. If the gutter is seamless, cut out the damaged section using a hacksaw. Place a scrap board in the gutter as shown to keep from bending the gutter as you cut.

2 Depending on the gutter type, you may slip the replacement piece inside it—in which case you should cut the replacement several inches longer than the opening. Or the piece can attach using a coupling, in which case you will need to shorten it. Use a wood scrap to hold the replacement piece firm while you cut it to length.

3 If one piece will fit inside another (as shown), be sure that the water will flow first over the inside piece and then down onto the outside piece. Use a putty knife or rasp to file away any burrs that would prevent a tight fit. Set the replacement in a generous bead of gutter caulk and drive screws or pop rivets to firm the connection.

WHAT IF… You need to remove a spike?

If a spike is installed too high or low, it should be removed so you can reinstall it correctly. Place a block of wood inside the gutter's upper lip as shown and use a scrap shim or other thin wood to protect the gutter as you pry out the spike.

STANLEY PRO TIP: Driving pop rivets

1 To drive a pop rivet, hold the two pieces tightly in position and drill a hole the required size. Slip the rivet into the hole.

2 Fit the insert into the pop rivet gun, slide it through the rivet, and squeeze the handle firmly. The two pieces will be drawn together, and the rivet will flatten out. It may take a couple of squeezes to fully tighten the rivet. Remove and discard the insert.

INSTALLING GUTTERS

Vinyl gutters are long-lasting, easy to work with, and readily available. You can find all the vinyl components you need at a home center or large hardware store. Vinyl gutters are sturdy enough to lean a ladder against. They may fade in color over the years but are not difficult to paint (see page 185).

Aluminum gutters are best installed by pros who have equipment that produces long, seamless sections that span the entire length of a house. They are rust-free but easily dented.

The wider the gutters and downspouts, the less likely they will clog or overflow in a heavy rainfall. If the old gutters worked well, buy gutters of the same size and type. Size recommendations for gutters and downspouts are based on three factors: the square footage of the roof that is served by the gutter, the pitch of the roof, and the expected rainfall intensity in your area. Measure the largest roof area that will be served by a gutter and downspout and ask a salesperson at a home center for advice on the correct gutter and downspout sizes.

1 On the fascia at the farthest point from the downspout, measure down from the drip cap ½ inch per 8 feet of gutter run or as recommended by the manufacturer. Snap a chalkline along the fascia and use a level to check the line for proper slope. Or use a line level to snap a level chalkline, measure down from it, and snap a guide line as shown. (Alternatively snap a line marking the bottom of the gutters as shown on page 183.)

PRESTART CHECKLIST

☐ **TIME**
Several hours to install about 100 feet of vinyl gutter, two downspouts, and six or seven fittings

☐ **TOOLS**
Chalkline, level, tape measure, drill, chop saw or hacksaw, putty knife

☐ **SKILLS**
Basic carpentry

☐ **PREP**
Remove the existing gutters and downspouts, remove all nails, inspect the drip-edge flashing, and make any needed fascia repairs.

☐ **MATERIALS**
Gutter sections and all required fittings, screws, seal lubricant, splash block

TYPICAL GUTTER COMPONENTS

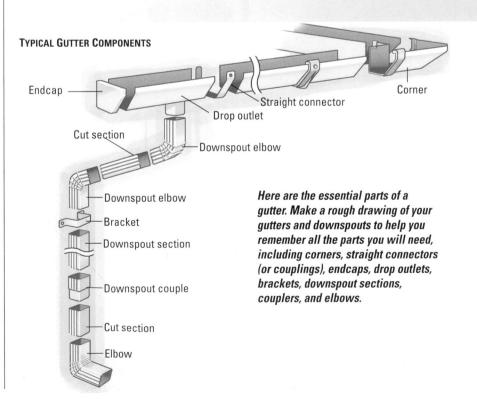

Here are the essential parts of a gutter. Make a rough drawing of your gutters and downspouts to help you remember all the parts you will need, including corners, straight connectors (or couplings), endcaps, drop outlets, brackets, downspout sections, couplers, and elbows.

2 Attach a drop outlet at the low end of the chalkline where you want the downspout to be. Depending on the location of the downspout, you may be able to simply add a cap to the drop outlet or you may need to attach a short length of downspout and then a cap.

3 Attach any outside corners, aligning them with the chalklines. Make sure they slope down toward the downspout. Drill pilot holes and drive screws into framing members if possible. Attach inside corners in the same way.

4 Attach the gutter brackets to the fascia; for extra strength drive long screws into rafter ends. Align the tops of the brackets with the sloped chalkline. Install three or four brackets for every 10 feet of gutter. (With some gutter types you will install the brackets first onto the gutters and then attach the gutters.)

WHAT IF…
You need a mid-run downspout?

Manufacturers recommend a downspout every 20 to 30 feet. If a run is longer than that, consider installing a downspout near the middle. Install the gutters on each side so they slope down to it.

STANLEY PRO TIP: **High-flow drop outlet**

If you live in an area that gets heavy rains or if your old gutters sometimes back up, consider installing high-flow drop outlets and extra-wide downspouts.

5 Measure the length of a run (from end to end or from an end to a corner), taking into account how far a gutter will insert into a corner fitting. Cut one of the gutters to length as needed and dry-fit all the gutter sections and the connectors. Once you are sure of the length, disassemble the parts. Apply seal lubricant to the rubber seals of the joints.

6 Slip the joints onto the gutters. Be sure to align them correctly so water will flow easily downhill. You may choose to assemble an entire run on the ground or just assemble some of the parts, install them onto brackets (next step), and assemble the rest of the parts in place against the fascia.

7 Working with a helper, position a workable length of gutter onto the drop outlet, brackets, and perhaps a corner. Check the alignment, then push the pieces together.

WHAT IF…
You attach with solvent?

Some systems attach together using cement, also called solvent, because it actually welds the pieces together (much as you would join PVC pipe). Dry-fit all the pieces and make sure they are the right lengths, then apply adhesive and join the parts. Once they have fully cured, the joints will be as strong as the plastic.

8 Drive screws through each gutter connector and into the fascia using the screw hole provided.

9 To cut a vinyl gutter, use a chop saw, a hand mitersaw with miter box, or a hacksaw (shown). After cutting use a knife or putty knife to scrape away all the burrs so the cut end can seat fully into a fitting.

10 Where a downspout needs to be offset from the end of a run, install a bracket near the end of the fascia. Cut a short section of gutter, attach an endcap, and attach to the drop outlet.

11 To measure for the length of downspout that reaches to the house wall, attach a 45-degree downspout elbow to the drop outlet. Hold another 45-degree elbow against the house. Slip a downspout section onto the second elbow and mark where it needs to be cut so it fits into the first elbow.

12 Cut the downspout sections to fit and attach them to the fittings using lubricant or cement, as needed. Leave about ¼ inch at each joint for expansion. Attach the downspout to the house near the elbow by slipping on a downspout bracket and driving two screws into siding or trim.

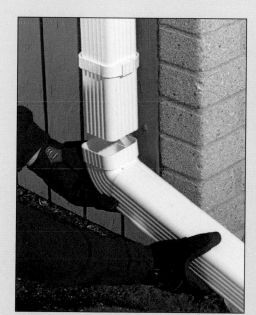

13 The elbow at the bottom of the downspout should be about 6 inches above grade or at the right height so the downspout extender (next step) will be sloped at a rate of at least ½ inch per foot.

14 At the bottom install a length of downspout resting on a plastic or concrete splash block. To further direct water away from the house, use a flexible extender.

STANLEY PRO TIP

Painting vinyl gutters

To paint vinyl gutters first clean them with denatured alcohol and a stiff brush or an abrasive pad. Then apply 100-percent acrylic paint. Or apply alcohol-base primer (also known as white shellac), then paint.

GLOSSARY

Architectural shingles: Composition or fiberglass shingles designed and textured to resemble wood shakes.

Asphalt: A dark, thick petroleum product used as a waterproofing material, sealant, and adhesive. Much roofing material is based on or uses asphalt.

Barge rafter: A rafter at the rake of an overhanging roof that does not rest on top of the walls. Barge rafters may be supported by the roof sheathing or on lookouts.

Batten: A narrow board that covers the joint between two pieces of siding, or a piece of applied trim that looks like a batten.

Building paper: A strong, thin paperlike material that prevents moisture from entering a building but allows moist air to pass through the wall from inside. Applied on the outside over the sheathing. Also known as house wrap or building wrap.

Built-up roofing: Roofing consisting of layers of asphalt, felt, and gravel. Frequently applied to flat roofs and especially used for commercial roofs in the past. The asphalt is melted and applied with mops. Modern materials such as EPDM or modified bitumen are better choices for residential use.

Clay tiles: Roofing tiles made of fired clay. A durable but expensive roofing material. Metal tiles are available that resemble clay.

Composition shingles: Roofing shingles with a felt or fiberglass base treated with asphalt and covered with mineral granules. These are the most common roofing material.

Counterflashing: Pieces of flashing that cover other flashings to provide a more weatherproof seal.

Course: A row of shingles or other roofing or horizontal siding. Roofing and horizontal siding courses overlap from top to bottom so water will flow down over the surface without getting behind it.

Cricket: A peaked structure behind a chimney to prevent buildup of snow and ice that could cause leaks. The cricket is built like a small roof and is covered with roofing.

Dormer: A structure on a sloping roof, usually with one or more windows, that has its own roof. A dormer room may be a sloped shed roof, a peaked roof, or a hipped roof. The dormer roof usually joins the main roof, and the sides require flashings.

Drip edge: A formed metal strip that goes under the shingles along the edge of a roof. The strip is shaped so water will form drops and drip off rather than being drawn under it.

Eave: The lower edge of a roof that overhangs the building walls. The underside of the an eave may be open or covered, and a trim board (see *Fascia*) is often attached along the edge.

EPDM: Ethylene propylene diene monomer rubber. A flexible, heavy synthetic rubber sheeting often applied to flat roofs. Durable and easier to install than built-up roofing.

Fascia: A trim board applied to the edge of the eaves. The fascia is usually perpendicular to the ground and covers the ends of the rafters. The edge of the sheathing may extend past the fascia. The drip edge under the roofing extends past the fascia so water will drip from the roof.

Felt: A nonwoven sheeting impregnated with asphalt, often called tar paper. Felt is available in 15-pound or 30-pound weights (the weight per 100 square feet) and is applied under roofing or siding to provide additional weather protection.

Fiber-cement: Siding material made of sand, cement, and reinforcing fibers. It is available in several forms, including strips for lap siding and panels.

Fiberglass shingles: Composition shingles with a fiberglass base or fiberglass-reinforced asphalt base. Fiberglass shingles are generally lighter and more durable than asphalt shingles.

Flashing: Sheet metal or plastic sheets or strips used to form waterproof seals between surfaces or around openings on a roof or wall. Some flashings are preformed for specific purposes.

Gable: The section at the end of a structure from the eaves to the ridge of the roof. A gable forms a simple triangle on a building with a peaked roof.

Hip: The junction between two sloping roof planes that have their eaves at an angle to each other. A hip makes an external angle, the opposite of a valley.

Lap siding: Boards or strips of siding applied horizontally in courses. Available in different widths, styles, and patterns, including shiplap, tongue-and-groove, and beveled. Lap siding may be made of wood, wood products, fiber-cement, metal, or vinyl.

Lookout: A framing member that extends a roofline beyond the gable end.

Modified bitumen: A flexible sheet material that is rolled over a roof and sealed to the roof and adjoining pieces with heat.

OSB: Oriented-strand board. A sheet material made from wood chips bonded together under pressure. Often substituted for plywood or boards as sheathing.

Panel siding: Siding material in the form of sheets, usually 4×8 or 4×9 feet. Panel siding can be smooth or textured and may have decorative grooves in the face. Edges are often tongue-and-groove. May be made of plywood, wood products, or fiber-cement.

Rafter: A structural member that runs from the ridge to the eaves to support the roof.

Rake: The edge of a roof at the gable end.

Ridge: The top edge of a peaked roof. Can also refer to the ridge beam or board that runs along the top of the rafters.

Roll roofing: Asphalt roofing in a continuous strip usually 36 inches wide. Often used for sheds and utility roofing; less durable than the heavier composition shingles.

Roof jack: Another name for the flashing or seal around a vent pipe through a roof.

Sheathing: Boards or sheet material such as plywood applied over wall studs or roof rafters to provide a base for siding or roofing. Older roofs covered with wood shakes or shingles were often built with open sheathing, boards spaced several inches apart.

Shed roof: A roof with a single plane that slopes in one direction.

Slate tiles: Roofing tiles cut from natural slate. Slate roofing is expensive and heavy but very durable.

Slope: The angle of a roof plane. It is often expressed in terms of the amount of rise over a 12-inch run: A 6:12 roof rises 6 inches for every 12 inches along the horizontal. Slope is sometimes expressed as "6-in-12."

Soffit: The underside of overhanging eaves. Soffits can be open or closed; closed soffits must have openings to allow air circulation for attic ventilation.

Starter strip: Roofing material applied as the first course along the eaves. Composition shingles can be trimmed to serve as the starter course.

Step flashing: Pieces of flashing that form a waterproof joint between the side of a chimney, dormer, or similar structure and the sloping plane of a roof.

Story pole: A board marked to show the courses of siding.

Stucco: A mortar-base siding material applied with a trowel.

Stud: The vertical structural member of a wall in a wooden frame building.

Tongue-and-groove: A joint treatment for siding in which the extended edge of one course or panel fits into a groove cut into the edge of the next course or panel.

Truss: An engineered, prebuilt assembly of rafters and other framing members to support a roof.

Valley: A junction between two sloping planes of a roof that forms a shallow V-shape interior angle or channel.

Wood shakes: Pieces of wood split from logs used for roofing or siding. Shakes are rustic and not particularly uniform.

Wood shingles: Pieces of wood sawn from logs used for roofing or siding. Sawn shingles are more uniform than split shakes.

WSU: Waterproof shingle underlayment, also called ice guard. An adhesive membrane placed under roofing along the lower courses, in valleys, or in other places that require more protection than standard roofing felt can provide.

INDEX

A

Adhesive, 15, 74, 117, 184
Air hose fastener, 24
Air vents. *See* Vents
Algae and fungus protection, 8
Aluminum coating, 90, 93
Aluminum gutters, 178–181, 182
Aluminum siding
    choosing, 108
    repair, 170–171
Ants, carpenter, 157
Architectural shingles, 8, 33
Asphalt shingle installation,
        28–53
    chimney flashing, 35, 52–53
    cutting shingles, 45, 48, 49
    dormers, 46
    drip-edge flashing, 32, 33, 40,
        43
    layout options, 44–45
    nailing, 46
    order of work, 31
    over existing shingles, 32–35
    pipe flashing, 35, 48–49
    preparation for job, 30–31
    ridgecaps, 35, 49
    safety, 29
    sheathing repair, 38–39
    tearing off old shingles, 31,
        36–37
    thickness of shingle, 33
    three-tab shingles, 44–49
    tools, 28–29, 30
    underlayment application,
        40–41
    valley, closed-cut, 43, 51
    valley, open metal, 42, 50–51
    valley, woven, 42, 52
    valley flashing, 33, 42–43,
        50–51
    vent installation, 31, 35, 43
Attic
    insulation, 63, 84, 96–97
    ventilation, 43, 82, 96–101

B

Battens, roof, 55, 70
Birdstop molding, 70
Blanks, 18

Board-and-batten siding
    installing, 144–145
    repair, 166
    trimming around, 114
Boot flashing, 18, 35, 64–65, 81
Brick molding, 105
Bricks, sealing, 95
Building codes, 8, 30, 40, 105
Building paper, 104, 105, 112
Butt joints, 81, 108, 121, 126, 129

C

Cap nails, 75, 112–113
Caps, chimney, 94
Car siding, 107
Caulk
    butyl, 170–171
    gutter, 15, 179–181
    options, 155
    roofing applications, 4, 51, 53,
        63–65, 73, 91–92, 94
    siding applications, 115–116,
        121, 123–125, 127, 135,
        140–141, 154–160, 164–165,
        168, 170–171, 173, 179
    smoothing lines, 155
    stucco, 173
Cedar
    lap siding, 106
    shingle panels, 142
    tongue-and-groove siding, 107
    trim, 114
Cedar shakes
    cleaning and sealing, 89
    damaged, 85
    description, 9
    installing, 56–61
    replacing, 89
Cedar shingles
    choosing, 109
    cutting, 138
    decorative, 136
    installing, 136–141
    repair, 167
Cement tile. *See* Concrete tile
        roof
Chalklines
    for roofing, 26, 41, 45, 49–51, 58
    for siding, 112, 121, 123–124,
        126–128, 130–132, 139,

141–142, 148–150
Chimney
    caps, 94
    cricket, 14, 53
    repairs, 94–95
    sealing bricks, 95
Chimney flashing, 14
    asphalt-shingle roof, 35, 52–53
    concrete tile, 69
    flexible, 69
    repairing, 94
Clapboards, 106. *See also* Lap
        siding
Clay tiles, 10
Clothing, protective, 25
Collar flashing, 72
Composition shingles, 8, 28, 44
Concrete tile roof, 11, 55
    cutting tiles, 71
    eave arrangements, 70
    flashing, 68–69, 70, 72
    installing, 68–73
    profiles, 68
    repairs, 91
    ridgecaps, 72–73
Contractor tape, 112
Corner caps, 170
Counterflashing, 14, 15, 18, 35,
        37, 53, 85, 94
Cricket, chimney, 14, 53
Cupping, 84
Cutout, 124
Cutting
    asphalt shingles, 45, 48, 49
    cedar shingle panels, 142
    cedar shingles, 138
    concrete tiles, 71
    faux tile, 67
    gutters, 181, 184
    metal roofing, 62, 65
    panel siding, 148
    tongue-and-groove siding, 129
    trim, 114–116
    vinyl siding and trim, 131
    wood lap siding, 123–125
    wood shakes, 57

D

Delivery of materials, 16, 17
Dents, filling, 171

Doors
    flashing, 105, 154
    installing cedar shingles
        around, 140
    installing shingle panesl
        around, 142
    jamb extenders, 111
    trim application, 117
    trim removal, 110
Dormers, 46
Downspouts
    installing, 185
    mid-run, 183
    sealing, 180
    unclogging, 178
Drip-cap flashing, 105, 113,
        120–121, 144–145, 154
Drip-edge flashing, 14, 18
    damaged, 176–177
    for asphalt-shingle roof, 32, 33,
        40, 43
    for concrete tile roof, 70
    inspecting, 174
    installing, 40
    for modified-bitumen roofing,
        75, 78
    removing, 37
    repairing, 92
    for reroof job, 32, 33
    for roll roofing, 80
Drop cloth, 20, 110

E

Eaves
    anatomy, 176
    flashing, 14, 68, 92
    repair, 176–177
EPDM (rubber) roofing, 11, 54,
        74, 90
Epoxy wood filler, 127, 158, 164
Extension cord, GFCI-protected,
        27

F

Fan
    gable, 101
    roof, 100
Fascia
    inspecting, 174
    repairing, 176–177

Faux shakes and masonry, 109
Faux tiles, 66–67
Felt, roofing
  ASTM 15, 112
  for cedar shake roof, 56
  description, 19
  function of, 12
  hip roof, applying, 40
  for modified-bitumen roof, 75
  for roll roofing, 80
  under siding, 112, 121, 128, 130, 166
  for tile roofs, 68
  for vertical metal roof, 62
Fiber-cement siding
  choosing, 106–107
  cutting, 126
  finishing and maintaining, 127
  installing, 126–127
  shingle panels, 109, 140
  shingles, 141
Fiberglass mesh, 93
Fiberglass shingles, 8
Filler
  autobody, 171
  wood, 127, 158, 164
Fire resistance, 8
Flashing, roof
  asphalt shingle installation, 32, 33, 35, 40, 42–43, 48–53
  blanks, 18
  boot, 18, 35, 64–65, 81
  chimney, 14, 35, 52–53, 69, 94
  collar, 72
  for concrete tile roof, 68–69, 70, 72
  counterflashing, 14, 15, 18, 35, 37, 53, 85, 94
  drip-edge, 14, 18, 32–33, 37, 40, 43, 70, 75, 76, 78, 80, 92
  eave, 14, 68, 92
  for faux tile roof, 66
  head wall, 69
  importance of, 82
  J-metal, 69
  lead, flexible, 69
  materials, 18, 92
  for metal roof, 62, 64–65
  for modified-bitumen roof, 75, 78, 79

pan, 69
pipe/vent, 15, 18, 32, 35, 48–49, 60, 64–65, 72, 93
rake, 14, 43, 64, 65, 92
removing, 37
repairing, 85, 87, 92–94
self-adhesive, 15, 18
for shake roof, 56
step, 15, 18, 35, 49, 52
types, 12, 54
valley, 14, 18, 33, 37, 42–43, 50–51, 60, 62, 68, 93
Flashing, siding
  around windows and doors, 105, 154
  at butt joints, 121, 126, 129
  drip-cap, 105, 113, 116, 121, 144–145, 154
  repairing, 154
  self-stick adhesive, 103, 105, 113, 115, 126, 128–130, 136, 142–144, 146
  Z-flashing, 121, 144–146, 151
Flat roof
  modified-bitumen roofing, 74–79
  repairing, 90–91
  surfacing options, 11
Framing, 104, 111
Furring strip, 142, 143, 144

G
Gables
  eave construction, 117
  fan, 101
  vents, 101
Gloves, 28
Glue, 164
Grinder, 126
Gutters, 15
  components, 182
  high-flow drop outlet, 183
  inspecting, 84, 174
  installing, 182–185
  leaf guards, 178
  repairs, 178–181
  slope, 180

H
Hammer, roofing, 26, 46
Hand seamers, 65
Hand shear, 126
Hand tools, 26
Harness, body, 25, 29
Hatchet, roofing, 26, 56–61, 71
Holes, filling, 164
Horsefeathers, 32
Hot-tar roof, 91
House wrap, 104, 105, 112

I
Ice dams, 12, 40, 84, 174
Ice-guard membrane, 19, 40. *See also* WSU (waterproof shingle underlayment)
Inspection, building, 30
Insulation
  attic, 63, 84, 96–97
  under modified-bitumen roofing, 74
  rigid foam, 111

J–K
Jamb extenders, 111
J-metal flashing, 69
Jig, spacing, 47, 138
Jointer tool, 95
Joints, sealing, 154–155, 179
Knee pads, 25

L
Ladder
  anchoring, 23
  roofing, 24
  safe use of, 22–23
Lap siding
  choosing, 106
  installing fiber-cement, 126–127
  installing horizontal wood, 120–125
  removing, 110
  repair, 164–165
Layout, siding, 118–120, 122, 137, 146
Lead paint, 159
Leaf guards, 178

Leaks
  locating and repairing, 86–87
  preventing, 14–15
Ledger, 147, 150
Level, checking for, 118
Level, water, 123

M
Magnet, nail, 20, 26
Masking tape, 161–162
Masonry sealant, 95
Masonry siding, 109
Mastic, 72–73
Materials
  caulks and sealants, 4
  choosing roofing, 6, 8–11
  choosing siding, 106–109
  delivery of, 16, 17
  ordering roofing, 16–17
  ordering siding, 108
Measuring roof area, 16–17
Metal-cutter nibbler, 62
Metal roofing
  cutting, 62, 65
  description, 10
  installing, 62–65
  insulating and sealing, 63
  noise, 10, 63
Mildew, on wood shakes, 85
Mineral spirits, 87, 155
Modified-bitumen roof
  description, 11
  installing, 74–79
  repairing, 90–91
Moldings, acrylic or urethane, 114
Mortar, 14, 35, 91, 94–95
Moss, on wood shakes, 85

N–O
Nailers, power and pneumatic, 6, 27, 28–29, 43–44, 46–50, 137
Nailing guide, 59
Nails
  cap nails, 75, 112–113
  driving hidden, 86
  removing, 86
  roofing, 19, 43
  for siding, 124, 128, 137
Nail set, 170

OSB (oriented-strand board) siding, 106–107

P

Paint and painting
  aluminum siding, 170–171
  brush use, 160–161
  lead, 159
  order of work, 160
  prepping surface for, 159
  priming, 160
  problems, 156–157
  removing, 159
  roller use, 161
  sprayer use, 162–163
  stucco, 161, 172–173
  trim, 161
  vinyl gutters, 185
Panel siding
  applying trim to, 114
  board-and-batten effect, 150
  choosing, 107
  cutting, 148
  damage, preventing, 147
  fiber-cement shingle panels, 140
  installing, 146–151
  layout, 118, 146
Pan flashing, 69
Permit, building, 30
Pilot holes, 118, 124, 128, 165
Pipe/vent flashing
  asphalt-shingle roof, 35, 48–49
  boot, 18, 35, 64–65
  cedar shake roof, 60
  concrete tile roof, 72
  function of, 15
  metal roof, 64–65
  removing, 32
  repairing, 93
Pitch, roof, 16, 17
Plane, 138
Plastic sheeting, 20, 40, 87, 110, 129, 162
Pliers, broad, 65
Plumb, checking for, 118, 121, 145, 147
Plywood, 19, 38–39, 87, 107, 111
Pop rivet, 181

Power tools, 27
Preacher, 129
Primer, 75, 107, 123, 125–127, 146, 160, 170
Professional help, 6
Propane torch, 76–77
Punch tool, 135

R

Rafters, 12, 30, 38, 176–177
Rain-screen siding, 102, 143
Rake flashing, 14, 43, 64, 65, 75, 92
Repointing, chimney, 95
Ridgecaps
  asphalt-shingle roof, 35, 49
  cedar shake roof, 61
  concrete tile roof, 72–73, 91
  faux tile, 67
  over ridge vent, 99
  vertical metal roof, 65
Ridge vents, 72, 96, 97, 99
Roll roofing, 9, 80–81
Roof anatomy, 12–13
Roof anchors, 25
Roof area, estimating, 16–17
Roof fan, 100
Roofing
  anatomy of roof, 12–13
  asphalt shingle installation, 28–53
  materials, choosing, 6, 8–11, 18–19, 54
  ordering materials, 16–17
  repairs, 82–101
  safety, 22–25
  site preparation, 20–21
  tools, 26–27
  water, protection from, 14–15
  weather conditions, 30
Roofing cement, 14, 15, 19, 33, 35, 48–53, 60, 67, 72–73, 80–81, 85, 87, 92–93, 94, 100, 179
Roof jacks, 24, 44
Roof repairs, 82–101
  chimney, 94–95
  diagnosis and triage, 82
  flashing, 85, 87, 92–94
  flat roof, 90–91
  identifying problems, 84–85

leaks, locating and repairing, 86–87
  shingle replacement, 88
  spot repairs, 87
  tile roof, 91
  ventilation, 96–101
  wood shake replacement, 89
Rotted wood, 158, 174, 176–177
Rust, 157, 178

S

Safety, 5, 21, 22–25, 29, 48, 102, 126, 159
Scaffolding, 22
Scarf joint, 121, 124, 177
Scraper, 159, 160
Screws, self-sealing, 65
Sealer
  for roofing, 4, 62–65, 89, 95
  for siding, 107, 114, 118, 123, 125, 129, 154–155
Seat, roofer's, 58
Shakes
  aligning, 58
  choosing, 57
  cleaning and sealing, 89
  cutting, 57
  installing cedar, 56–61
  replacing, 89
  sizes, 56
Sheathing, roof
  for cedar shake roof, 56
  function of, 12
  repair, 38–39
  skip, 56
  solid, 56
Sheathing, siding
  materials, 104
  repairing, 111, 166
  rigid foam insulation, 111
  wood, 121
Sheet siding, 107. See also Panel siding
Shims, 165
Shingle panels
  cedar, 142
  fiber-cement, 140
  installing, 142
Shingle ripper, 27, 36–37

Shingles, roof
  asphalt shingle installation, 28–53
  carrying safely, 21, 23
  cupping, 84
  cutting asphalt, 45, 48, 49
  damaged, 84
  layers, number of, 31
  loose, 87
  protecting, 21
  repairing broken, 33
  replacing, 88
  tearing off, 31, 36–37
  thickness, 33
  types, 8–9
  warranty, 8, 9
  wood, 56
Shingles, siding
  cedar, 109, 136–141, 167
  choosing, 109
  cutting, 138
  fiber-cement, 141
  removing, 110
  wood, 114
Shovel, roofing, 27, 36–37, 110
Siding
  installation, 118–151
  materials, choosing, 106–109
  materials, ordering, 108
  over existing siding, 111
  preparing for, 102–117
  profiles, 111, 128
  removing, 110
  repair, 152–173
  sealing, 118, 129
  slipping flashing/felt under, 35, 41, 49
  trim application, 114–117, 129
Siding installation, 118–151
  board-and-batten, 144–145
  cedar shingles, 136–141
  fiber-cement lap siding, 126–127
  horizontal wood lap siding, 120–125
  layout, 118–120
  panel, 146–151
  rain-screen siding, 143
  shingle panels, 142
  tongue-and-groove, 128–129
  vinyl, 130–135

Siding repair, 152–173
  aluminum siding, 170–171
  board-and-batten, 166
  dents, filling, 171
  filling holes, 164
  lap siding, 164–165
  painting, 160–163
  paint problems, 156–158
  preparation for painting, 158–159
  preventing damage, 152
  rotted wood, 158
  sealing joints, 154–155
  shingles, 167
  stucco, 172–173
  vinyl siding, 168–169
Sister joist/rafter, 30, 38
Site preparation, 20–21
Slate tiles, 9
Slope, roof, 16, 17
Soffit
  inspecting, 174
  repairs, 176–177
  vents, 96, 98
Solvent, 184
Spackle, 160
Sprayer, paint, 162–163
Square, checking for, 123
Standoff stabilizers, 23
Staples, 43, 112, 137
Steel siding, 108
Step flashing, 15, 18, 35, 52
Story pole, 118–120, 122, 128, 130, 137, 142
Stucco
  choosing, 109
  repair, 172–173
  texture, 173
  tinting and painting, 161, 173
Stud spacing, 104
Surform tool, 138
Swing stick, 122, 137

T
Tar-and-gravel roof, 11
Tarpaper, 19, 40. *See also* Felt, roofing
T-bevel, 125, 141, 145
Termites, 157

Tile roof
  faux tiles, 66–67
  installing concrete, 68–73
  repairs, 91
Tin snips, 42, 62, 65, 121
Tongue-and groove siding
  choosing, 107
  installing, 128–129
Tools, roofing, 26–27, 28–29, 30
Trash, dealing with, 20, 36, 110
Trim
  applying, 114–117
  board options, 114
  butt-jointed window, 116
  cedar shingles, 137
  corner, 129
  cutting, 114–116
  decorative, 132
  under eaves, 117
  inside corners, 115
  installing molded trim boards, 117
  miter-cut window, 116
  outside corners, 114–115
  over siding, 115
  painting, 161
  removing, 110
  sealing, 114
  vinyl siding, 132–135
  windows and doors, 110, 116–117
Trusses, 12
T 1-11 siding, 107

U–V
Underlayment, 40–41, 85. *See also* Felt, roofing; WSU (waterproof shingle underlayment)
Valley
  closed-cut, 42–43, 51
  open metal, 42, 50–51
  woven, 42, 52
Valley flashing, 18
  asphalt-shingle roof, 33, 42–43, 50–51
  cedar shake roof, 56, 60
  function, 14
  removing, 37
  repairing, 93

tile roof, 68
  vertical metal roofing, 62
  vinyl, 33
  W-shaped, 33, 68
Vapor barrier, 143
Vent flashing. *See* Pipe/vent flashing
Ventilation
  anatomy of flow-through, 96
  attic, 96–101
  fans, 43, 82, 100, 101
Ventilation tape, 72, 73
Vents
  gable, 99, 101
  installation, 31, 35, 43, 98–101
  removing, 32
  ridge, 43, 99
  roof vents, 31, 35, 43, 97, 100
  soffit, 98
  vent options, 97
Vertical metal roofing. *See* Metal roofing
Vinyl gutters, 175, 178, 182–185
Vinyl siding
  choosing, 108
  cutting, 131
  installing, 130–135
  materials, 130
  profiles, 111
  removing, 110
  repair, 168–169
  thickness, 130
  trim, 132–135

W–Z
W-valley flashing, 68
Wall flashing, 49, 69
Wall structure, 104
Warranty, shingle, 8, 9
Waste removal, 20, 36, 110
Water damage, 85
Water level, 123
Water table, 121–122, 144–145
Weep holes, 130
Windows
  flashing, 105, 154
  glazing, 157
  installing cedar shingles around, 140

installing shingle panels around, 142
installing wood lap siding around, 125
installing vinyl siding around, 132–133
painting, 161
pretrimmed, 116
sealing rough opening, 113
trim application, 116
trim removal, 110
Wood filler, 127, 158, 164
Wood hardener, 158
Wood rot, 158, 174, 176–177
Wood shakes and shingles
  for roofing, 9, 56–61, 85, 89
  for siding, 106, 107, 109, 136–141, 167
WSU (waterproof shingle underlayment)
  for asphalt shingle roof, 33, 40, 48
  for cedar shake roof, 56
  description, 19
  high-temperature, 62
  at valley, 41, 42, 43
  for roll roofing, 80
  for tile roofing, 68
  for vertical metal roofing, 62
Z-flashing, 121, 144–146, 151

KNOWLEDGE IS THE BEST TOOL

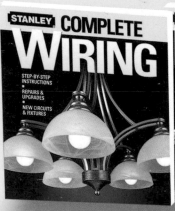 STANLEY COMPLETE **WIRING** — STEP-BY-STEP INSTRUCTIONS • REPAIRS & UPGRADES • NEW CIRCUITS & FIXTURES

CONSTRUCT

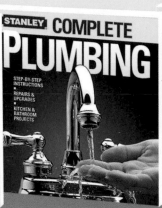 STANLEY COMPLETE **PLUMBING** — STEP-BY-STEP INSTRUCTIONS • REPAIRS & UPGRADES • KITCHEN & BATHROOM PROJECTS

REJUVENATE

 STANLEY COMPLETE **Tiling** — STEP-BY-STEP INSTRUCTIONS • FLOORS, WALLS & COUNTERTOPS • DECORATIVE PROJECTS

PLAN & REPAIR

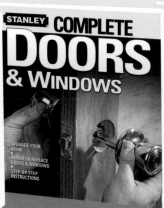 STANLEY COMPLETE **DOORS & WINDOWS** — UPGRADE YOUR HOME • REPAIR OR REPLACE DOORS & WINDOWS • STEP-BY-STEP INSTRUCTIONS

ENHANCE

 STANLEY COMPLETE **PAINTING** — PAINT ANY SURFACE • INTERIORS AND EXTERIORS • STEP-BY-STEP INSTRUCTIONS

MAINTAIN

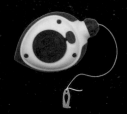